D1027632

The Women of Izmaelovka

A Soviet Union Collective Farm in Siberia

Alexey Vinogradov
Albert Pleysier

UNIVERSITY PRESS OF AMERICA,® INC.
Lanham • Boulder • New York • Toronto • Plymouth, UK

Copyright © 2007 by
University Press of America,® Inc.
4501 Forbes Boulevard
Suite 200
Lanham, Maryland 20706
UPA Acquisitions Department (301) 459-3366

Estover Road
Plymouth PL6 7PY
United Kingdom

Library of Congress Control Number: 2006939171
ISBN-13: 978-0-7618-3722-0 (clothbound : alk. paper)
ISBN: 10: 0-7618-3722-1 (clothbound : alk. paper)
ISBN-13: 978-0-7618-3661-2 (paperback : alk. paper)
ISBN-10: 0-7618-3661-6 (paperback : alk. paper)

∞™ The paper used in this publication meets the minimum
requirements of American National Standard for Information
Sciences—Permanence of Paper for Printed Library Materials,
ANSI Z39.48—1984

The book is dedicated to the women
who shared with the authors their life stories.

Contents

Preface

Izmaelovka is a village located on the steppes of the Ural region in Siberia. According to legend, the land on which the village was built belonged to a Turkish man name Izmail. In the eighteenth century the land and the surrounding areas were taken from the Turks and settled by Russians. The new settlers farmed the land, raised cattle and built the dwellings that became Izamaelovka.

The village was turned into a collective farm after collectivization was enforced in 1929. The people who became members of the collective were forced to relinquish their lands and farm machinery and much of their livestock. Their possessions became property of the collective, which belonged to the State. The wealthier peasant families identified as Kulaks were not granted membership; they were rounded up and carted off to places unknown. During collectivization, the village church was closed, and its icons were removed and destroyed. The Russian Orthodox priest was taken away by the authorities, and the worship of God, thereafter, was forbidden.

Collectivization and the removal of religion are two of many developments that would affect the lives of seven women who are residents of Izmaelovka. The women are the subjects of this book and as they recount their lives they discuss Joseph Stalin's acts of repression, the Great Patriotic War, de-Stalinization, Nikita Khrushchev's agricultural programs, the Brezhnev years and the fall of the Communist Party. They describe their education and work, their kitchen gardens and homes, their activities in the Village Club, the village traditions, the seasonal changes and the different stages of life. The ideological .influence that the Communist Party brought into Izmaelovka through socialist competitions, propaganda and the youth organizations is also described by the women. Through indoctrination they were taught that a good Communist was a person who was honest, just in action and hard working and that through Communism a better life and society would be achieved in the Soviet Union.

The women experienced different and similar events. The perspective of each woman is unique, and their jobs varied. They worked as milkmaids, pig herders, tractor drivers, combine operators, nurses, librarians and Village Club coordinators. They worked hard and long days. They had little control over their lives and destinies and were forced to sacrifice and sacrifice some more. They suffered from sadness and despair, and periodically they would experience moments of joy.

One of the earliest events that would influence the women of Izmaelovka was Tsar Nicholas II's abdication from the Russian throne during World War One. Thereafter, the reigns of power in Russia were held by a provisional government created by Russia's parliamentary body called the Duma. This temporary government was removed by Vladimir Lenin and his Bolsheviks. They were Marxian socialists who eventually called themselves Communists, but they did not immediately build a socialist state. Following Lenin's death a struggle for power took place among the leadership within the Communist Party, and by 1928 Joseph Stalin had become the preeminent figure within the Party. He believed that it was necessary to transform the Union of Soviet Socialist Republics, the Soviet Union, into a true socialist state. He and the Party would begin to do this with the first of several five-year plans. All agricultural land in the Soviet Union was placed under State ownership and management. The small peasant farms were made into large collective farms, and the large privately-owned landed estates were turned into state farms. As a result, the peasants living in Izmaelovka witnessed their small land holdings brought together as one collective farm. All of these developments had such a significant impact on the lives of the women of Izmaelovka that the authors felt it was necessary to record them in the Introduction of the book.

Acknowledgements

No one entered Izmaelovka without the permission of Mr. Alexander Zaplatin, the director of Izmaelovka. His invitation and hospitality were essential for the research of this book. Upon his request, Pavlina Ribakova, the Village Club coordinator, introduced the authors to the seven women whose life accounts are the subject matter of the book.

The portrait on the cover of the book is of a young Russian woman. She along with millions of other women was forced by the Communist leadership of the Soviet Union to labor long-hour days under difficult circumstances. As a female worker, her face conveys the soul of the women of Izmaelovka. On the collar of her simple blouse she wears the Komsomol pin that bears the likeness of Vladimir Lenin, the father of Communist Russia. The portrait was drawn by Jane Pleysier and used with her permission.

Finally, the authors wish to thank Katherine Plotnikova, Klavdia Vidvina, Juliana Selezneva, Maria Grigorievna, Nina Kozhevnikova, Anna Kostomarova and Valentina Nenasheva for sharing with them their life stories.

Introduction
"The Prelude to Collectivization"

At the dawn of the twentieth century, Russia was a politically authoritarian and economically backward power. The Romanov dynasty headed by Tsar Nicholas II regarded itself as a divine right monarchy, ruling with the help of a large bureaucracy and an army that was used toward territorial conquest and against rebellious subjects. A secret police that had made Siberia notorious as the site for Russian penal colonies kept down dissent, but opposition against autocracy could not be quieted. Liberals, desiring to bring about political, social and economic reforms through peaceful and legal avenues, and revolutionaries, using terrorism, sought to overthrow autocracy. The revolutionaries looked mostly to the Russian peasantry as their army of revolution, and in the early nineteen hundreds the peasants as well as Russia's industrial workers would help bring about the fall of Russia's autocracy.

The people of imperial Russia faced major problems in the latter years of the nineteenth century. The peasant population increased more than fifty percent between 1861 and 1900, mostly as a result of a high birthrate and a declining death rate, but the increase in the peasant population meant a reduction in individual peasant land holdings. At the same time, Russia experienced the growth of a large-scale machine industry, which resulted in the emergence of a small, urban working class. Since industrialization was new to Russia, its workers labored under working conditions that were both unsafe and unhealthy. Wages were low, and the average workday in a mill was from twelve to fourteen hours. The poor treatment from which the workers suffered filled within them a feeling of deep discontent and militant consciousness.

In 1904-1905, Russia's imperial designs in eastern Asia culminated in a disastrous war against Japan. The Russo-Japanese War began with a Japanese surprise attack on the Russian naval squadron at Port Arthur in February 1904. Russia had leased Port Arthur from China in 1898 as part of its expansion into East Asia and Manchuria. For years these moves had troubled the Japanese, and Russia had neither kept its promises to withdraw nor acknowledged Japan's proposal for establishing mutually acceptable spheres of influence. The war and the initial patriotism the war evoked was welcomed by the tsar and his government. The war, however, was a disaster for Russia. In December 1904, the Russians surrendered Port Arthur and this was followed by Russian defeats in Manchuria and the annihilation of a large Russian fleet in Japanese waters.

When the accounts of Russia's military defeats reached St. Petersburg, the workers in several factories in the capital city went on strike. A priest named George Gapon, hoping to deflect the workers from revolutionary ideas, urged the workers to petition the tsar to end the war, convene a constituent assembly, grant civil rights and establish an eight-hour workday. On Sunday morning, January 9, 1905, Father Gapon led a group of industrial workers from various parts of the city toward the Winter Palace, the home of the tsar and his family in St. Petersburg. The marchers carried icons and sang "God save the tsar." As the petitioners approached the Winter Palace, they were ordered to halt. When they disregarded the order, the commander of the tsar's troops ordered his men to fire on the peaceful demonstrators. More than one hundred people were killed, and many more were wounded.

The news of Bloody Sunday undermined the people's faith in the tsar and united them against autocracy. Throughout the empire the massacre caused an angry uproar culminating in labor unrest, peasant insurrections, student demonstrations and mutinies in both the army and navy. Peasants, organizing themselves at the village level, discussed seizing the property of their landlords. Urban workers joined together in organizations that called for a general strike. The people who participated in the strike demanded a democratic republic, the release of political prisoners and the disarming of the government police. Most business and government offices were closed, and Russia's economic life came to a halt.

The tsarist government managed to restore order in the fall of 1905 after agreeing to make political reforms. In October 1905, a month after the Treaty of Portsmouth ended Russia's war with Japan, the tsar issued a manifesto that promised full civil liberties, a constitution and the creation of the Duma—an elected legislature with the power to enact laws. The October Manifesto was supposed to transform autocratic Russia into a constitutional monarchy. The constitution, which went into effect in 1906, stated that for a measure to become a law it had to be passed by the delegates in both houses of the Duma; however, the tsar retained absolute veto power. The tsar would also determine the duration of the Duma's sessions, and he had the right to dissolve it at will if he set a date for new elections. Article 87 within the constitution allowed the executive to rule by decree. After the revolutionary crisis had passed, the tsarist government returned to its reactionary ways and restricted the authority of the Duma.

World War One hastened the decay that had been eating away at tsarist Russia for decades. In August 1914, Germany declared war on Russia. Initially, the declaration of war produced unity and patriotic resolve in Russia. Virtually the entire Duma pledged to support Russia's war efforts and voted for war appropriations. The people believed that the war was being fought to defend Russia, and in the cities Russian patriotism became anti-German. The capital city was renamed Petrograd because its former name, St. Petersburg, sounded too German. The Russian high command dispatched two armies into Germany's eastern Prussia, but the push forward was only temporary. The German army responded quickly and with their allies, the Austrians, drove the Russians out of Germany, through Poland and back into Russia. Hundreds of thousands of Russian soldiers lost their lives, and Russian morale was seriously damaged. In the fall of 1915, Tsar Nicholas II left Russia's capital city to take personal command of the Russian armies.

In his absence from the capital city the tsar placed effective control of the Russian government into the hands of his wife, Alexandra. By this time the tsarina had fallen under the influence of Grigori Rasputin, a semiliterate Siberian monk. To Alexandra, Rasputin was a holy man for he alone seemed able to stop through hypnosis the bleeding of her hemophiliac son, Alexis. Rasputin's influence over the tsarina made him an important power behind the throne, and he did not hesitate to interfere in government affairs. Ministers were appointed and dismissed on a word from Rasputin. By late 1916, Rasputin's behavior had become so intolerable that three members of the high aristocracy, fearful for the survival of the monarchy, murdered the monk. His death would not make a difference; by this time public confidence in the tsar's government had disappeared. Two years of Russian military defeats, millions of military casualties, shortages of food and fuel in the cities and government inefficiency and corruption had turned the people against the crown.

In March 1917, a series of strikes and demonstrations would bring to an end tsarist rule. In the month previous, the government had introduced bread rationing in Petrograd after the price of bread had soared. Many of the women who stood in lines waiting for bread were also factory workers who labored twelve-hour days. On March 8, a day celebrated since 1910 as International Women's Day, thousands of Petrograd women marched through the capital city demanding "Peace and bread" and chanting "Down with autocracy." Soon the women were joined by other workers, and together they called for a general strike that succeeded in shutting down, on March 10, all the factories in the city. The tsarina informed her husband about these developments in a letter, and the tsar responded by demanding the adjournment of the Duma and ordering the police and the troops stationed in Petrograd to disperse the striking crowds by shooting them if necessary. At first the soldiers obeyed, but soon a significant number of them joined the demonstrating crowds. On March 12, some members of the Duma formed a provisional committee to keep order. Hostility toward the crown and demonstrations against the government had already spread to other cities. Alone and helpless, Nicholas II followed the advice of his generals and abdicated on March 15 in favor of his younger brother, Michael. He in turn abdicated in favor of the Duma's provisional committee. By this time the members of the committee considered themselves a provisional government. The three hundred year reign of the Romanov dynasty ended, and Russia ceased to be a monarchy.

At first the Provisional Government enjoyed considerable support both at home and abroad. It disbanded the tsarist police, granted amnesty to political prisoners and allowed exiles to return home. It repealed all limitations on freedom of speech, press and association. It abolished laws that discriminated against ethnic or religious groups. It announced plans for social reforms and promised to summon a democratically elected constituent assembly that was to establish a permanent government by giving Russia a constitution. Russia's allies recognized almost immediately the Provisional Government as the legitimate governing body of Russia and began to supply it generously with war credits.

The two most important issues facing the Provisional Government were agrarian discontent and the continuation of the war. Russia's peasants wanted land, and they wanted it immediately. The Provisional Government, however, believed in acting with deliberation and according to the law. It refused to sanction peasant seizure of land despite the increasing disorder in the countryside. Instead, it appointed a commission to collect data on which future agrarian legislation was to be based. It was a decision that was inadequate to the emergency. As to the war, the members of the Provisional Government continued to honor the tsar's commitments to Russia's allies by participating in the fight against Germany and its allies. Most of the members hoped that Russia would win the war and gain the territories that had been promised to Russia.

The Provisional Government was also faced with the demands of the soviets and socialists. The soviets were councils consisting of deputies representing the people who had elected them. The soviet of Petrograd was formed in March 1917, but at the same time soviets were organized throughout Russia in army units, in factories, in work shops and in the rural areas. The soviets represented the more radical interests of the lower classes and were largely composed of socialists of various kinds.

The Socialist Revolutionaries were the most numerous of the socialist groups. They concerned themselves with the burdens of the peasants. They wished to establish peasant socialism by seizing the great landed estates and creating rural democracy. Since the beginning of the twentieth century, the Socialist Revolutionaries had come to rely on the use of political terrorism to accomplish their goals.

Since 1893, Russia also had a Marxist Social Democratic Party. It divided in 1903 into two factions, the Mensheviks and Bolsheviks. The Mensheviks believed that Russian socialism would grow gradually and peacefully and that the tsar's government should be replaced by a democratic republic in which the socialists would cooperate with bourgeois political parties. Working under a democratic system, the socialists would gradually become the dominant political force and would organize a socialistic society through parliamentary means. They would not resort to crime or undemocratic methods to attain their goals. The Bolsheviks, the other faction, advocated the establishment of socialism through revolution. This faction was under the leadership of Vladimir Ilyich Ulyanov who would become better known by his underground alias, Vladimir Lenin.

Lenin was born into a middle-class family in 1870. He received a legal education and became a lawyer. In 1887, he turned into a dedicated enemy of tsarism when his older brother was executed for participating in a plot to assassinate the tsar. Lenin's search for a revolutionary faith led him to Marxism, and in 1894 he moved to St. Petersburg where he organized an illegal group known as the Union for the Liberation of the Working Class. Arrested for this activity, Lenin was sent as a political prisoner to Siberia. After his release in 1900, he chose to go into exile in western Europe and eventually assumed the leadership of the Bolshevik faction of the Russian Social Democratic Party.

Under Lenin's direction, the Bolsheviks became a party dedicated to revolution. Lenin believed that only a violent revolution could destroy a capitalist system, and the revolt must be carried out under the leadership of a small party of well-disciplined professional revolutionaries. Between 1900 and 1917, Lenin spent most of his time in Switzerland. There he lived a lonely existence and developed his theoretical view of the special role a militant party should play in a country that, like Russia, was just achieving modern capitalism. The party, he argued, could achieve its aims only by recognizing the revolutionary potential in the peasants' desire for land. Lenin hoped one day to return to Russia to recruit the peasants in a revolution that would establish a socialist state patterned on Marxist ideology.

When the Provisional Government was formed in March 1917, Lenin believed the opportunity for the Bolsheviks to seize power in Russia had come. In April 1917, the German High Command, calculating that Lenin's agitation would disrupt and undermine Russia's war effort, arranged to transport him in a sealed train through Germany to the Baltic Sea coastline. From there he could be brought by ferry to Finland. Lenin, his wife and several trusted colleagues eventually arrived in Russia by way of Finland. Shortly after their arrival, they were joined by other Marxists the tsarist government had formerly imprisoned or who had been forced to flee abroad.

In a series of proposals known as his "April Theses," issued on April 20, 1917, Lenin presented a blueprint for revolutionary action. In the "April Theses," Lenin maintained that the soviets of soldiers, workers and peasants were ready made instruments of power. The Bolsheviks must work to gain control of these groups and then use them to overthrow the Provisional Government. At the same time, Bolshevik propaganda must seek mass support through promises directed to the needs of the people: an end to the war; the redistribution of all land to the peasants; the transfer of factories and industries from capitalists to committees of workers; and the relegation of political power from the Provisional Government to the soviets. Three simple slogans summed up the Bolshevik program: "Peace, Land, Bread," "Workers Control of Production" and "All Power to the Soviets."

In late spring and early summer the Provisional Government struggled to maintain control of Russia. The Provisional Government promised that a constituent assembly, called for in the fall of 1917, would confiscate and redistribute royal and monastic lands. The promise was meaningless since many peasants had already started in March to seize and divide up the estates of Russia's large landowners. People in the cities, suffering from rising inflation and dwindling food supplies, were becoming more discontented. Disorder in the factories rose as workers, demanding higher wages, organized strikes and engaged in industrial sabotage.

The military situation was also deteriorating. The Petrograd soviet had issued its Army Order No. 1 in March to all Russian military forces encouraging them to remove their officers and to replace them with committees composed of "elected representatives of the lower ranks" of the army. Army Order No. 1 ended the government's control over the army, and it led to the collapse of all military discipline. When the Provisional Government attempted to initiate a new military offensive against the Germans in July, the army simply dissolved. Masses of peasant soldiers, hungry, ragged and disgruntled, deserted their units and returned home to their native villages to join their families in seizing lands.

At the same time the influence of the Bolsheviks in Russia continued to grow. By the end of October, the Bolsheviks were the majority in the Petrograd and Moscow soviets. The number of Bolshevik members had increased from 50,000 to 240,000. Meanwhile reports of unrest abroad convinced Lenin that the world was on the threshold of a proletarian revolution, and he decided that the time had come to overthrow the Provisional Government. Although he faced opposition within the Bolshevik ranks, he managed to gain support for his decision. He was especially fortunate to have the close cooperation of Leon Trotsky.

The Bolshevik takeover of political rule in Russia came relatively easy. Lenin and Trotsky organized a Military Revolutionary Committee within the Petrograd soviet to plot the overthrow of the government. Beginning on November 4, large demonstrations and mass meetings were addressed by Trotsky. On the evening of November 6, Bolshevik forces seized railroad and communication centers, post offices, electric power plants and other key places in Petrograd. At noon the next day they stormed the Winter Palace, the headquarters of the Provisional Government, and arrested or put to flight all the government's cabinet members. The Provisional Government had fallen almost without resistance. In less than a day the Bolsheviks had carried out successfully their political revolution.

On the afternoon of November 7, Lenin announced to the National Congress of Soviets in Petrograd that he was transferring the political sovereignty of the Provisional Government to that body. The National Congress of Soviets represented the local soviets from all over the country. Lenin then maneuvered the National Congress of Soviets to accept the Council of Peoples' Commissars as the executive body of the new government. The Bolsheviks occupied the top positions in the Council of Peoples' Commissars. Lenin held the post of chairman, and Trotsky was in charge of foreign affairs. Lenin pledged to build a socialist state and to end Russia's war with Germany.

In the first months, the Bolsheviks built the rudiments of a new order. Lenin nationalized all landowners' estates and turned them over to local rural soviets. The action legitimized the peasants' previous seizure of land and assured the Bolsheviks of peasant support. Lenin also met the demands of urban workers by turning over control of mines and factories to committees of workers. All imperial institutions were dismantled, and all social titles and military ranks were abolished. A campaign was initiated against the Russian Orthodox Church, an institution the Bolsheviks regarded as an ally of the tsar and an enemy of socialism. The church hierarchy was destroyed, and its lands, buildings, utensils and vestments were nationalized. The debts incurred by the tsarist government were repudiated, a decision that angered the foreign governments that had provided funds to Russia before and during the war.

Confident that the majority of Russia's people favored their policies, the Bolsheviks allowed elections by universal male suffrage for a constituent assembly to be held. However, they were shocked when they learned that they polled about a quarter of the vote while their main adversaries, the Social Revolutionaries, polled more than sixty percent. The delegates elected to the constituent assembly met only once, on January 18, 1918. The following day Lenin dissolved it by decree and sent guards bearing rifles to prevent it from ever meeting again. The anti-Bolshevik majority in the constituent assembly was furious at Lenin's act of pure force against the popular will, but there was no public outburst and the delegates did disband.

One of Lenin's primary goals was to end Russia's war against Germany. He started peace negotiations with the Germans in December 1917. The Germans, aware of Russia's helplessness, demanded among other things, Finland, the Ukraine, eastern Poland and the Baltic provinces. If Germany's demands were met, Russia would lose more than a million square kilometers of territory, including a third of its arable land, a quarter of its population and three-quarters of its deposits of iron and coal. Lenin balked at Germany's demands, but with the German military advancing into Russia and the Russian army disintegrating, he believed that he had no other option but to agree to the demands. The treaty that took Russia out of the war was signed at Brest-Litovsk on March 3, 1918. Nine days later Lenin moved his government to Moscow, the center of Russia.

After the signing of the Treaty of Brest-Litovsk, Russia plunged into a civil war. Throughout Russia there emerged groups that were hostile to the Bolsheviks who now called themselves the Russian Communist Party. Lenin changed the name of his party in 1918 because the word communist implied a concern for the human community. The counterrevolutionaries, collectively called "Whites," were led by former tsarist military officers and included members of the outlawed nobility, former landowners, supporters of the tsar and socialists from rival parties, including the Mensheviks and Socialist Revolutionaries. By late June 1918, Russia's allies of World War One intervened in the Civil War on behalf of the opponents of the Communists. The Japanese occupied Russia's far eastern provinces, while the French, Americans and British sent supplies as well as troops to aid the White forces. The Allies were eager to see the Whites win the Civil War, not only to prevent the spread of Communism but also because they hoped that under different political leadership Russia would reenter the war against Germany. To meet the new danger, the Communists hastily formed the Red Army in the summer of 1918. Under the leadership of Leon Trotsky, the Commissar of War, the Red Army became a well-organized formidable fighting force. Trotsky reinstated the draft and even recruited and gave commands to former tsarist army officers.

He insisted on rigid discipline; soldiers who deserted or refused to obey orders were executed.

Between 1918 and 1921, the Red Army was forced to fight on many fronts. The first serious threat to the Communist regime came from Siberia where a White army under Admiral Alexander Kolchak pushed westward and advanced almost to the Volga River before being stopped. Attacks also came from the Ukraine in the southeast and from the Baltic regions. In mid-1919, White forces under General Anton Denikin swept through the Ukraine and advanced almost to Moscow, Lenin's new capital. At one point in late 1919, three separate White armies were closing in on the Communists. They were eventually pushed back, and by 1920 the major White forces had been defeated and the Ukraine had been retaken. The next year, the Communist regime regained control over the independent nationalist governments in the Caucasus: Georgia, Russian Armenia and Azerbaijan.

The Communists were equally successful in crushing political opposition in the territories under their control. Following a failed assassination attempt on Lenin, the Communists initiated a Red Terror campaign. It was conducted by Felix Dzerzhinsky, the chief of a newly organized secret police force, the All-Russian Extraordinary Commission for the Struggle Against Counterrevolution and Sabotage, known by its acronym of CHEKA. They arrested, tried and executed anyone known to be or suspected of being hostile to the Communists. The place of enemies, in Lenin's words, was "against the wall." CHEKA killed as many as two hundred thousand opponents of the regime. The most famous victims were the Tsar Nicholas II and his entire family, who were executed in Ekaterinburg in July 1918. In order to prevent organized opposition, Lenin's government outlawed all political parties except the Russian Communist Party and thereby converted Russia into a one-party dictatorship.

During the Civil War, Lenin instituted a policy known as War Communism. It was introduced in 1918 to deal with plummeting agricultural and industrial production, soaring inflation and rising hunger in the cities. Under War Communism the government nationalized transportation and communication facilities as well as banks, mines, factories and businesses that employed more than ten workers. The land holdings of poor peasants were exempted from confiscation, but the Communists did seize grain from peasants to feed the people in the cities and the soldiers in the Red Army. The peasants were left with only a bare minimum for subsistence.

Socializing the Russian economy would help the Communists win the Civil War, but it would also bring the country to the brink of collapse. The government's program of requisitioning food so alienated the peasants that many grew only enough food for their immediate needs. Added to this development was a drought, which caused a great famine between 1920 and 1922 that claimed the lives of as many as five million people. The socialization of the economy brought chaos to Russia's industries and mines as well. Many workers appointed to managerial positions lacked experience and this caused industrial output to fall. By 1921 it was only 21 percent of the 1913 level. Many industrial workers moved from the cities to the rural areas in search of employment. Transportation systems broke down and Russia's exports shrank to a fraction of the 1917 level.

Lenin made an ideological retreat to prevent the collapse of Communist Russia. In March 1921, he adopted the New Economic Policy, also known by its initials as NEP, which was a compromise between socialist and free enterprise practices. Lenin described it as "a step backwards in order to take two steps forward," a temporary measure that would be abandoned as soon as the economy stabilized. Under the New Economic Policy the State retained control over large industries, mines, banking, transportation and communication facilities and foreign trade. It did, however, permit private local trade and restore small shops and factories (those with fewer than twenty workers) to their former owners. Under the New Economic Policy a peasant still had to pay a governmental tax, which was a fixed portion of his crop yield, but he was allowed to sell the remainder of his crop to the State if he wished or to a private purchaser if he preferred. Within limits, a peasant was permitted to lease additional land and hire labor. Peasant agriculture became capitalist once again, and the profit motive was brought back. Concessions were also made to foreign entrepreneurs who wanted to exploit the mines and oil wells in Russia. By 1928, the measures under the New Economic Policy had brought industrial and agricultural production back to pre-war levels.

The Communists, while coping with Russia's economic problems, formalized their authoritarian rule in a constitution drafted in 1924. The constitution granted the franchise to all productive workers over the age of eighteen but not to the bourgeoisie or those closely identified with tsarism and the Russian Orthodox Church. The Party leadership demonstrated their distrust of the peasants by making each urban vote of the electorate equivalent to five rural votes. Ostensibly, political power rested with the elected local soviets that were organized according to occupation. These soviets elected delegates to the congress of soviets of their canton, the smallest administrative unit, and each of these congresses in turn sent delegates to a congress at the next administrative level. The system, which continued up through a series of steps to the All-Union Congress of Soviets, allowed considerable control from the top. Because the All-Union Congress of Soviets was not a permanent body, the members elected an executive committee to act in their behalf between sessions, and the executive committee appointed the Council of People's Commissars. The constitution did not mention the Communist Party, but the

Party was the real center of political power. The Party's Central Committee elected the small Politburo (political bureau), and this body made all the major policy decisions for both the Party and the government. The constitution recognized some union republic rights, including the right to secede, but by the time the Union of Soviet Socialist Republics was officially formed the Communist Party was firmly in power in all of the republics, and it would not permit them to secede.

The Union of Soviet Socialist Republics was commonly called the Soviet Union. It was formally established in December 1922 as a federal union consisting of territories, regions, nominally autonomous states and republics. Of the four republics, the Russian Soviet Federated Socialist Republic (Russia) was the largest and the most influential. The other three were the Transcaucasian Soviet Federated Socialist Republic, the Ukrainian Soviet Socialist Republic (Ukraine) and the Belorussian Soviet Socialist Republic (Belorussia). As time went on the boundaries of the republics would shift and the number of republics would increase.

Lenin died on January 21, 1924, and following his death there emerged the cult of Lenin. Inspired by genuine reverence and by a political desire to move the masses around a potent symbol, the members of the Politburo had Lenin's body embalmed and placed in a sarcophagus inside a mausoleum for public viewing. The mausoleum, designed as a cube-like structure and made of red granite, was built on Red Square in front of the Kremlin Wall in Moscow. Outside of the mausoleum a large number of people daily would stand in line for hours to enter and view the mummified body of Lenin. The writings of Lenin became sacred and irrefutable. Images of the father of the Soviet Union appeared everywhere in stone and metal, on canvas and in print. Lenin corners, analogous to the icon corners of Russian Orthodoxy, became fixtures in nearly every Soviet institution, and Lenin's name graced thousands of collective and state farms, libraries, schools and streets. On January 25, 1924, just five days after Lenin's death, Petrograd was renamed Leningrad.

There were several members in the seven-man Politburo who desired to succeed Lenin as leader of the Communist Party, and one of these men was Joseph Stalin. Born Joseph Dzhugashvili in 1879 in the Georgia region of Transcaucasia, Stalin was the son of a poor shoemaker. Admitted to a seminary to be trained for the priesthood, young Stalin was later expelled for holding radical opinions. He joined the Bolsheviks in 1903 and came to Lenin's attention after staging a daring bank robbery to obtain funds for the Bolshevik cause. In 1912, Lenin made Stalin a member of the Bolshevik's Central Committee and in that same year told him to write a work on Marxism and nationalism, which Stalin completed to Lenin's satisfaction. In 1917, Stalin arrived in Petrograd about three weeks before Lenin and worked as editor of the Bolshevik paper, Pravda. In 1922, he became General Secretary of the Communist Party's Central Committee. As General Secretary he prepared the agenda for Politburo meetings, supplied the documentation for points under debate and passed the decisions down to the lower levels. He controlled all Party appointments, promotions and demotions. He saw to it that local trade unions, cooperatives and army units were directed by Communist bosses who were responsible to him. He had files on the loyalty and achievements of all managers in industry and of all Party members. Stalin's key administrative post in the Party apparatus gave him an enormous advantage in the struggle to take Lenin's place.

Stalin won the struggle for power, and as leader of the Communist Party he would use his position to transform the Soviet Union into a socialist state. Lenin had been forced to retreat from socializing the Russian economy because of the chaos that had been brought on by the Civil War. He had instituted the New Economic Policy and through it had succeeded in rescuing Russia from an economic crisis. The crisis was past and Stalin, who remained committed to the Communist dream, now wanted to remove from the Soviet Union all forms of capitalism. He began the process in 1928 by ending the New Econmic Policy and launching the first of three five-year plans. Its goals were to eliminate all elements of capitalism, to increase agricultural production through mechanized collective farming and to develop large-scale industries.

The implementation of the first two goals would begin after the Kulaks through their actions created food shortages. Under the New Economic Policy private ownership and free enterprise were permitted to flourish in the Russian countryside to ensure enough food for the workers in the cities. A number of land owning farmers had become so prosperous that they had the means to hire labor and lend money within their villages. The Communist Party called them Kulaks, an old derisive term used to describe grasping merchants and usurers. During 1928 and 1929, the Kulaks and other farmers withheld grain from the market because agricultural prices were too low. It caused food shortages in the cities which resulted in potential unrest. Sometime during these difficult months, Stalin decided that agriculture must be collectivized to produce sufficient grain for food and export and to free peasants for labor in factories.

In late 1929, Stalin declared that the Kulaks were to be eliminated as a class. He accused them of trying to sabotage the State by withholding grain and threatening the cities with famine. Stalin's actions against the Kulaks were part of the State's plan to erase the private ownership of land and to collectivize farming. The Kulaks probably numbered less than five percent of the rural population, but in time a Kulak was identified as any peasant who opposed Stalin's policy. Party agents were sent into the countryside to expropriate the land and farm equipment owned by the Kulaks. The victims were then rounded up and deported to forced labor camps or to desolate regions in Siberia. Perhaps some 2,000,000 households, as many as 10,000,000 people, suffered this fate.

Peasants who were not expropriated were pressured to become members of newly created collective farms. Joining a collective meant that a peasant family was required to give up their land, their farm equipment and all of their livestock except for one milk cow, geese and chickens. Many peasants cherished their plots of land and wanted no part of collectivization. In desperate revolt, they burned their crops, smashed their equipment and killed and ate their cattle rather than turn them over to the State. More than half of the horses in all of the Soviet Union, forty-five percent of the cattle and two-thirds of the sheep and goats were slaughtered. Millions of peasants left the land and moved to the cities. Their lands lay uncultivated, and over the next four years famine would kill millions of people.

The peasant resistance persuaded Stalin to call a brief halt to collectivization in March 1930. He justified the slowdown in an article entitled "Dizzy with Success." In it he blamed the consequences of the process on local Party officials who had been too eager to rush through the program. By contradicting his own order of a few months before, Stalin managed to escape some of the hatred that would otherwise have been directed at him. Stalin further decided that collectivization should be voluntary.

The State soon resumed its coercive collectivization program. By the end of the first year of the First Five-Year Plan about fifty percent of the farms in the Soviet Union had been collectivized. An additional ten percent were added during the next three years so that by 1933 sixty percent of the farms were collectivized. The number would rise, and by 1939 more than ninety-six percent of the farms in the Soviet Union were collectivized. In 1941, there were 250,000 collectives supporting 19,000,000 families.

A collective farm (kolkhoz) was a community of farmers in a stated area that included a store, a school, a library, a hospital and a clubhouse. It was created by combining small farms into one farm. The average size of a collective farm was 5,900 hectares (14,573 acres). The land used by the farm belonged to the State, and it was leased to the collective in perpetuity. Theoretically, it was a self-financed cooperative venture carried out by its members but in fact it was governed by the State's regulations, a rural soviet and district officials. The members of a collective elected the farm's managing committee and a chairman. The farm chairman was usually a Party member, and he was nominated by the Party. It was the chairman who oversaw the production of goods to meet the production goals determined by the State's planning boards. He was also to provide ideological leadership for the members of the farm. The chairman that did not meet ideological purity requirements was removed.

The income of a collective farm member was determined by the number of workday credits that she or he earned. Work performed rather than hours expended was the basis for awarding credits. A tractor driver, for example, might have earned three workday credits for plowing a hectare (two and one half acres) of land in ten hours, but a less skilled farm hand might have received only one workday credit for the same number of hours of work. Workday credits for each farm member were added up at the end of the year, but the distribution of money and produce was made to each member after the collective farm's debts had been paid and after certain obligations had been satisfied. The collective farm was required to pay taxes to the State. The farm's leadership also had to set aside funds that would be needed to rent machinery, buy livestock, construct buildings, purchase seed and feed and provide the members of the farm with educational and cultural activities. If the year's harvest had been abundant, the members of the collective farm would live quite well. If the harvest had been poor, they would suffer.

During the Stalin years the collective farms were required to turn over a large percentage of their produce to the State. The State purchased the produce at fixed prices, and the State set the prices. The State then charged higher prices when it sold the produce to the consumers in the towns and cities. Sometimes the price that was charged for an agricultural product in a city store was substantially higher than what a collective farm had received for it. The markup in price helped the State finance the industrialization of the Soviet Union.

The State assisted and controlled a collective farm through the supply of heavy agricultural equipment furnished by a Machine Tractor Station (MTS). Collective farms were not permitted to have their own tractors or combines; they were required to rent them from a station located nearby. The collective farm paid the Machine Tractor Station for the use of the machines in produce, not in money, and this produce went to the State since the Machine Tractor Station was owned by the State. Technicians at the station repaired during the winter months the machinery that was returned to the station following a harvest season. They were also at the service of a collective farm for advice regarding fertilizer, irrigation, crop rotation and other agricultural matters. Administrators of a Machine Tractor Station could directly affect the success of collectives by deciding when and to whom to allot tractors and how many tractors to allot. The good will of the station administrators was of utmost importance to a collective farm.

Stalin's collectivization campaign also included the creation of state farms. A state farm (sovkhoz) was quite distinct from a collective farm. The state farms were created through confiscation by the State of large landed estates, and the average size of a state farm was 15,300 hectares (37,791 acres). A state farm was exclusively a State enterprise. It was given production goals, and the operating budgets were determined by the State's planning agency. The entire output of the farm was delivered to the State's procurement agency. The state farm workers were employees of the State. They were paid a salary and were guaranteed a minimum wage. An employee of a state farm worked, as a rule, a forty-six hour week and was paid overtime. There were no Machine Tractor Stations associated with state farms; each had its own permanently available mechanized agricultural equipment.

A family in a collective farm and in a state farm was assigned a private plot of cultivable land. The plot, usually called a kitchen garden, was generally between one-fourth to one-half a hectare large. On this land the family was entitled to grow vegetables for their own consumption and to raise livestock. A family was permitted to own one cow and two calves up to two years of age, one sow and a litter of pigs, ten sheep or goats and an unlimited number of poultry. The family was allowed to sell on the free market whatever they grew or raised on their private plot. A family was also allowed to own a dwelling place and minor implements, and the entire homestead could be sold or left by will to the owner's descendants.

The collective farms and state farms would experience some changes following their formation. In 1958, for example, the Machine Tractor Stations that had given the Communist Party some control over the collective farms were disbanded. Each collective farm was required to purchase its own tractors and combines and any other agricultural machinery. In 1965, the State decided that a collective farm worker must be guaranteed a minimum wage, a pension and other benefits. Two years later the State decided that each state farm was to become a self-financed entity, which in theory the collective farms had been since their creation. At the same time a number of collective farms were being joined together and converted into state farms, a process that had begun in the 1950s. In 1990, a year before the Communist Party would fall from power, there were some 52,000 large farms in the Soviet Union, 55% of them were collective farms and 45% were state farms. Together they accounted for up to 75% of the gross value of agricultural output in the Soviet Union. All the garden plots which made up only three percent of the country's arable land, produced nearly twenty-five percent of the Soviet Union's total agricultural harvest.

Izmaelovka was turned into a collective farm in 1929. Collectivization was organized and carried out when men representing the Communist Party arrived in the village. The wealthy peasant farmers and their families were taken from their homes and transported out of the Ural region to another area in Siberia. These people were forced to leave behind virtually all of their possessions. The people who remained living in the village became members of the newly created collective farm, which was Izmaelovka. Each family continued living in their place of residence, each was allotted a small kitchen garden and each was permitted to own one cow, several sheep and goats and chickens and geese. Those who worked on the farm were paid with food, and the amount of food that they received was determined by the number of workdays for which they were given credit. The standard of living for most of the people in Izmaelovka was low.

Life for the people of Izmaelovka began to improve after the collective farm was made a part of a large state farm. It was in 1964 when this was done. Thereafter, the people were recognized as employees of the State; they were paid for their work in wages and were guaranteed a minimum wage. Throughout the 1970s the people's standard of living continued to rise. More consumer goods and a greater variety items became available in the village store. The more prosperous workers purchased these items as well as the consumer goods that were sold in the nearest cities such as Magnitigorsk. Some families had the financial means to purchase a motorcycle or a car. The increasing improvement ended in the latter 1980s. Suddenly the shelves in the village store became empty, and the Soviet currency lost its value. Once again the standard of living for the people of Izmaelovka declined.

In the early 1990s Izmaelovka became a corporation. It happened after the Communist Party fell from power and the Soviet Union was dismantled. The native inhabitants of the village were given ownership of the farm and the farm's economic activities were entrusted to a body of directors. Each share holder received from the farm's directors a monthly income in accordance to her or his share holding. Among the native inhabitants were Katherine Plotnikova, Klavdia Vidvina and Maria Murzina, three women who have shared with the authors their life stories. The life stories of Juliana Selezneva, Nina Kozhevnikova, Anna Kostomarova and Valentina Nenasheva are also recorded in the book. These four women are also residents of Izmaelovka but they were born elsewhere. They moved to Izmaelovka after it became a collective farm.

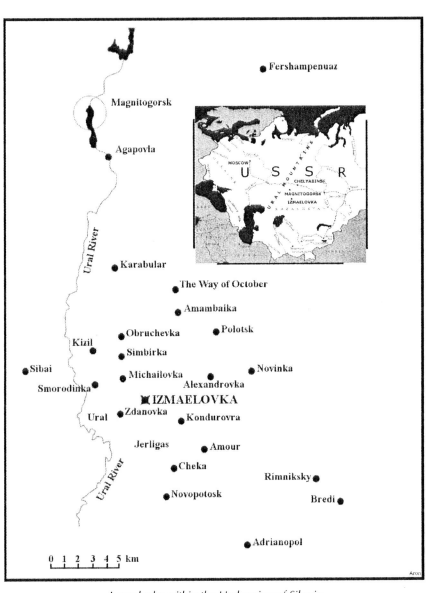

Izmaelovka within the Ural region of Siberia

Chapter One

"Old Survivor"

Katherine Plotnikova (Babakatja)

Babakatja is a native of Izmaelovka and one of its oldest residents. As a teenager she witnessed the enforcement of the collectivization policy. In Izmaelovka it was carried out by representatives from the Communist Party's regional headquarters located in the nearby community of Kizil. Babakatja remembers the fate of the more wealthy farmers in the village and of those people who opposed collectivization. She believes that many who agreed to become members of the newly formed collective farm did so out of fear that they would suffer severe consequences if they refused to join.

The Communist Party placed burdensome taxes on Izmaelovka. The collective farm was required to give to the State a large percentage of its annual harvest of wheat. The wheat that the collective farm was permitted to keep was divided among the members of the farm in direct proportion to the number of days that each worker labored. As a young woman, Babakatja worked as a wagon driver whose job it was to bring the harvested wheat to a state storage area located in another community. The task would take several months and was completed during the winter season. It was one of many jobs to which Babakatja was assigned by those who managed the farm.

Izmaelovka became a farming enterprise after the Communist Party fell from power in 1991. Babakatja was given ownership over several hectares of land, and since then the directors of the enterprise have paid Babakatja for the use of her land. With the annual payment that she receives along with her state pension, Babakatja is able to pay her expenses and purchase from the village store all she needs. Babakatja no longer works except when she is called upon to prepare for burial the body of a person who has died in the village. As a form of relaxation she will sit at her small spinning wheel and sing as she spins wool from sheep raised in Izmaelovka into thread. Her ancestors were Cossacks and she applies the name to herself.

BABAKATJA'S ACCOUNT

According to legend, the land on which our village was built belonged to a Turkish man. His name was Izmail and that is why the people who built the village named it Izmaelovka. The Russians settled here after this land and the surrounding areas were taken from the Turks in the eighteenth century. The Russian settlers turned the virgin lands of the steppes into agricultural fields. They planted crops, raised cattle and built the dwellings, which became Izmaelovka.

The collectivization of Izmaelovka was preceded by several visits to the village by men from Kizil. These men collected information on the rich farmers and on the Cossack men who had fought during the Civil War. They wanted to know if a Cossack had served in a White army. They inquired if there were any former Cossack soldiers who had fled from Russia to China after the Red Army victory (see Glossary—Cossack).

After the gathering of information, the authorities from Kizil carried out a policy of expropriation. The richest farmers of the village, the so-called Kulaks, were deprived of their possessions. Many of these people were taken away. We did not know where they were brought. We did not learn about their fates until much later when we were told that some were sent to the wild virgin lands located in the Caucasus, and some lived in Uzbekistan. There were other rich farmers who fled from the village to avoid being sent away; they abandoned their houses, their possessions and their lands.

My father was a Cossack who fought in the Civil War. At the beginning of this war all the Cossacks from the Kizil region, including my father, fought for the White forces. They were captured by the Reds, and as prisoners of war they were lined-up by the Red officers and given an ultimatum. Those who wanted to join the Red Army were told to ride their horses a short distance to the right. My father guessed that anyone who did not join the Reds would be imprisoned and so he advised the others to ride to the right as the Red officer had advised. All the Cossacks joined the Red Army. After that the men were sent to a bathhouse and were given new uniforms. Father told my mother later that the men had been wearing old worn-out uniforms furnished by the Whites, and they were happy with the new uniforms. Father would return home in his Red Army uniform after the war was over. Because father had fought for the Reds and because our family was not wealthy, our possessions were not expropriated.

During the period of expropriation, the Kalmiks in Izmaelovka disappeared. The Kalmiks were Turks who lived along the outskirts of the village. They worshipped as Orthodox Christians, went to church as we did, married in the church and celebrated the Orthodox holidays. They wore different clothes. They had black hair and dark narrow eyes. They spoke the Russian language fluently, but they also used a different language with each other. They associated with us in a friendly manner, but they never married Russians. They were required to serve in the Russian Army, and when World War One broke out many of the adult males were sent to the front. The wives of these men would often discuss the war with the village women whose husbands were also soldiers. During the period of expropriation, the Kalmiks disappeared. Their large wooden houses stood empty. I do not know why they disappeared, and I do not know where they went.

Following the disappearance of the Kalmiks, authorities from Kizil came to speak to the people in the village. Izmaelovka, at the time, had an administrative board, and the members of the board arranged for the village people to assemble in the village school building. At the gathering the authorities from Kizil informed the people that they would have to convert their village into a collective farm. They said it was better for them to work together as a group and to divide the harvest in a just manner among all the workers of the farm. They told the people to keep a record of how many days each person worked in a year. At harvest time all the crops would be divided in direct proportion to the number of days the people had worked. Many questions were asked during the meeting. Some people wondered why they should cooperate with the authorities. Others wanted to know what life would be like on a collective farm. The authorities assured the people that their way of life would be no different except that it would improve as the standard of living was raised.

When two or three important men representing the regional administration arrived from Kizil to enforce collectivization, everybody in the village was afraid. The representatives arranged a meeting and insisted that everyone in the village join the collective farm. They assured the people that they would enjoy a good life on the collective and promised that there would be economic equality for everyone. The promise was not convincing, yet the villagers became members of the farm realizing that if they did not join they would suffer the consequences. One family after another entered the collective; they joined out of fear.

The men representing the regional administration knew that if they did not enforce collectivization quickly and effectively, they would suffer terrible repercussions. They too were working out of fear. When Stalin gave the order to create collective farms, the order was obeyed. No one dared go against Stalin's directives. "What would you do?"

After joining the collective, the families were required to drive their animals to an area designated as the collective farm yard. Many bulls, horses and cows were driven to the yard. Each family, however, was allowed to keep one cow. I was thirteen years old when this happened.

During collectivization the village priest was arrested, and church worship services were stopped. Agents of the political police arrived in a car on a Sunday while the priest was conducting a worship service. They took the priest, placed him in their car and drove away. The old women attending the worship service cried out "What are you doing?"

After the arrest of the priest, outsiders came to the village and destroyed the church as a place of worship. First they gathered in a large pile the church accessories and small icons (see Glossary-icon). They then burned them. They did this in front of the church. I remember looking at the old people who were watching the acts of destruction. They warned those who were burning the icons not to "touch these gifts of God." After that the strangers began taking the larger icons out of the church. They did not burn these because someone pointed out to them that the wood on which the icons had been painted was good quality wood. Later these icons were used to make the small beds for the village kindergarten.

The church building was converted into the Village Club, and thereafter it was used as a storage building for seeds. After Izmaelovka became a state farm the former church was dismantled, and the wood of the building was taken away.

During the campaign against religion my mother wrapped the family icon of a crucified Jesus Christ in a cloth and hid it in a chest. It was kept there for a long time. When I removed something from that same chest years later, my son noticed the icon and asked me what it was. "This is our crucified Jesus Christ," I answered. "Let me keep it," he said. I gave him the icon. He cleaned it, and now it is on display in an honored place in his home.

Today there are people in the village who worship God and celebrate the religious holidays. For almost seventy years the children born in the village were not baptized. Their names were written in books kept by the Village Council. Now, some people bring their children to Kizil and have them baptized in a church. Maybe sometime soon the village will again have a beautiful church.

Shortly after the enforcement of collectivization several young people in the village moved to Magnitogorsk. The State was turning Magnitogorsk into a huge industrial center and the industrial enterprises in that city needed many young workers (see Glossary-Magnitogorsk). Men from Magnitogorsk came to Izmaelovka several times to recruit young workers. They promised the young people good jobs. Those who went to the city became industrial workers. The young people who chose to stay in the village lost the opportunity to leave and became old, like me, working the land.

Working on the collective farm during the early years of its existence was hard but rewarding. Plowing the soil with bulls was difficult. Being small in stature, I was forced to ask a plowman to help me put the yoke on my bull every workday. Once that was done I would drive the bull with my whip. I found that the bull was obedient, and I discovered that driving a bull is easier than working with a horse.

When we harvested I would usually couple my mowing machine to three horses. I would sit on the seat of the machine and operate it with a foot pedal. Whenever I would see a large stone, I would lift the mower with my pedal, pass over the stone and then lower the mower again. When the grass was very dense, I would whip the horses to go faster so that the mower would cut faster. The horses would go very fast. Mowing was hard work, but we were rewarded with good harvests.

The harvests on the steppes today are not as good for two reasons. The tractors that are used today are much stronger than the bulls we used. With those tractors the workers are able to plow deeper bringing the clay underneath the fertile soil to the top, but wheat does not grow well in clay. In the 1930s we would leave an agricultural field fallow for several years before planting it again with wheat. Today the agricultural fields are not left fallow, and the intensive use of the fields have exhausted them. It is another reason why the yields at harvest time have successively diminished.

Much of the wheat grown by our collective farm was demanded by the State and had to be delivered to a designated location where it was stored. After the grain was harvested, it was first brought by wagon train to Amour. It was left there until the winter, and after the snow covered the ground the grain was brought with sleds to the state storage near the Bredi railway station.

A wagon train that brought the grain from Izmaelovka to Amour consisted of fifteen to twenty wagons. Each wagon had a large box that had been placed on a flat bed with four wheels. The wheels were made of wood. They had wooden hubs, wooden spokes and wooden circles covered with iron hoops. A box would hold a ton of wheat, and after it was filled a person would sit on top of the grain and drive the two bulls pulling the wagon. The wheat was not covered because the collective farm did not have a tarpaulin or any kind of covering that would protect the grain from rain or wind. The lead and end wagons were usually driven by men, and the wagons in between were usually driven by women or young girls. It was done this way because it was believed that the men were better drivers. At night the men had less difficulty staying awake, and if a female driver should fall asleep it did not matter because her bulls would continue to follow the wagon in front of them.

I was one of several girls who were assigned to the wagon train brigade that was to bring the grain the collective farm had stored in Amour to the Bredi railway station. Before we left for Amour we placed many empty sacks in the wooden boxes that had been used to bring the grain to Amour. Now, however, the boxes were resting on sleds instead of on wagons. It was winter, and snow covered the ground so it was easier to pull the boxes on sleds than on wagons.

In Amour the collective farm had rented a house that we would use for several months. Here we were to sleep and to eat. We were expected to sleep on the floor in our clothes and cover ourselves with our padded jackets. In the mornings we would eat a breakfast that had been prepared for us by the wife of the owner of the rented house. She would prepare the flour, meat and potatoes that we had brought with us from Izmaelovka.

After breakfast we would first fill the empty sacks with the grain that had been stored in Amour and then begin our journey to the Bredi railway station. We would drive the bulls all day until we reached Rimenka in the evening. In this community the collective farm had rented another house for us. I remember the owner of this rented house distinctly. She was a kind woman who had great sympathy for us. She would prepare breakfast early in the morning and then awaken us telling us how sorry she was that she had to get us up. After breakfast we would hitch up the bulls and begin our twelve kilometer (7 mile) trip to Bredi, our final destination. It was usually cold, around 40 degrees, too cold to be sitting on the grain in the boxes so we would get out of the boxes and walk next to the sleds that were being pulled at a slow pace by the bulls.

At the state storage in Bredi we emptied the sacks filled with wheat. Sometimes the men in charge of the state storage wanted the wheat in large piles; sometimes they wanted it brought to a special drying tower. Carrying the heavy sacks of wheat to the top of the drying tower was difficult especially for girls. After we emptied our sacks, the leader of the brigade would give the state storage office an invoice, and then we headed back to Rimenka.

Upon our arrival in Rimenka the owner of the rented house was waiting for us with either soup or a meal of noodles. We unhitched the bulls and then went inside the warm house to eat our hot meal. It was so delicious, and we would get so sleepy. Meanwhile the homeowner's son would take the bulls and feed them hay. Others would bring the bulls water, and by the time the bulls had been fed and watered, we were asleep. The following morning we were awakened to return to Amour for more wheat, which was to be brought to the state storage in Bredi.

It took several months to bring to Bredi all the wheat the collective farm had stored in Amour. It was in March when we returned home to Izmaelovka. By this time our skin was raw and chapped because of the frost and cold weather.

One year several of us girls in the wagon brigade bought cloth and made for ourselves under garments. We were able to buy the cloth after we returned to Izmaelovka. I bought enough fabric to stitch together two underpants, but wearing them at first proved painful. The fabric rubbed against my hips, which were inflamed by the frost. "Oh my Lord that hurt!" However, we were determined to wear the under garments and not to be embarrassed again by an old woman who lived in Amour. She was the mother of the friend of our brigade leader and, knowing that the girls in our brigade did not own underwear, would call us "the army without pants." When the woman called us "the army without pants" the following year, our brigade leader corrected her and told her that this was no longer true. Our life was a life of few possessions.

The wheat the State permitted the collective farm to keep was divided among the members of the farm. The division was made in direct proportion to the number of days that each person had worked. For example, one year we received 8 kilograms of wheat for each workday. There were also years when we received only 3 or 5 kilograms of wheat for each workday. Of course the women workers did not receive as much as the male workers because the men did the more difficult work. Later on, during the war years, when almost all the men in the village were gone and the women worked at the more difficult jobs, the women received more for their workdays.

In 1937 my mother's brother was arrested by the NKVD (see Glossary-NKVD). The people in the village knew each other well, and in the depths of our souls we believed that the accusations which led to the arrest of my uncle and the arrests of other men in the village were contrived. However, a law had been passed which gave the NKVD the authority to arrest, to torture and to execute people. We knew that the NKVD had been ordered to execute many people. Did the NKVD agents want to execute people who were sentenced to death? It is impossible to say. No one protested the arrests because everyone feared for their life. At that time the sight of a NKVD agent would make a person's flesh crawl. "What good would it have done to publicly condemn the NKVD and denounce its actions?"

I learned about fascist Germany's attack on Soviet Russia on June 22, 1941. It was Sunday, and I had just returned to the village from a trip by wagon train to get oat seeds for planting. As I entered my parents house, my mother cried out, "Katja, Katja, we are in war." "What war and how will this war affect us?" I asked. I did not know what a terrible experience the war would be for us. Mother then took my two little sisters and me and walked to the river where my father was shepherding to tell him about the war. He was shocked by the news and alarmed. He feared that he would be forced to fight in another war.

The draft notices arrived at the village post office shortly after we learned about the war. When a man received his call-up papers he was expected to stop whatever he was doing and present himself immediately to the authorities. Therefore, when our family was informed that my brother's draft notice had arrived, we were alarmed because we knew that he was away from the village bringing wheat in a wagon train to a state storage. The trip to the state storage took several days. We informed the collective farm leaders about my brother's absence, and they immediately sent someone to overtake the wagon train to order my brother to get to the Military Registration and Enlistment office in Kizil. My brother arrived in Kizil the following day and on time. If he had arrived late, he would have been punished.

From Kizil my brother and the many other village men who had been drafted were loaded on trucks and taken to the military front. They were brought through Magnitogorsk and on to Chebarkul where they remained for several days. I was told that my father and my Uncle Sergei, who had also been drafted, were in Chebarkul at the same time that my brother was there, but they never had the opportunity to see and talk to my brother. From Chebarkul they were sent to different places along the military front.

During the war, the women in the village would receive letters from the men who were fighting along the front. A letter was written on a small sheet of paper that had been folded in a triangular shape. It would have a stamp bearing the words "soldier's free letter" meaning that the sender did not have to pay to have the letter delivered to its destination. The soldiers would write that they were still alive and that they hoped the family members at home were doing well. They never wrote about the fighting or about their friends or enemies or about their clothes or meals. There was not enough room on the small sheet of paper to write about such things. A typical letter would read "I am writing this letter on my knee to let you know that I am still alive."

My father was killed somewhere in the Ukraine, and we eventually received a vikluchka announcing his death. We in the village condemned Adolf Hitler for the death of my father as well as the deaths of the other men who were killed during the war. Unfortunately, life is not without sorrow, and our lives have been filled with sorrow and grief. Following my father's death, mother received from the State a little money to help her care for my two younger sisters (see Glossary—vikluchka).

Michael, my brother, survived the war. He remained in the army for a while and was stationed in the Far East. When he was diagnosed with tuberculosis he was told by doctors to return to the dry climate of his homeland. After his return to the Ural region in 1955, he worked as a traffic officer. He was a kind person. Everybody liked him. He was strict but just. He used to ask me who I thought would die first, him or me. He never celebrated his sixtieth birthday, and I believe that this was due to his war injuries.

Two days after the war was announced, I and several other girls from Izmaelovka were sent to Obruchevka to be taught how to take care of a tractor. Some other girls were sent to Verkhneuralsk to learn to operate a combine.

None of us were asked if we wanted to do this. We were simply summoned by the Village Council and were told that they had received a letter informing them that a number of girls within the village would have to learn to be tractor drivers and combine operators. The members of the council had chosen us. Later the Village Council sent several girls to Kizil to learn to drive trucks.

While living in Obruchevka, we occupied a house that was rented by our collective farm. There were some eight girls in the house. The collective farm provided us with food, and the cook who lived with us prepared our meals. The cook had children and so there were more than ten people sleeping in one room. The cook would awaken us early each morning to feed us a breakfast that she had prepared on a Holland stove.

The period of study and training lasted one month. At first we listened to lectures that were given by our instructors. Then we were brought to the garage and taught to apply what we had learned in the classroom. "But what can you really learn in one month?" Well I learned the difference between petrol and diesel fuel, and I learned how to start a tractor engine. "But that was all I learned, nothing more."

I was afraid of the tractor. I saw it as a huge iron beast, which could injure me. The tractors during the war had four iron wheels, two small ones on the front and two large ones on the rear. The rear wheels had iron studs. In order to start a tractor engine a handle had to be turned to crank it. It was difficult to start the engine using diesel fuel, and we had no gasoline. Once when I tried to start an engine, the handle did not fully turn but instead snapped back and injured my arm. Fortunately, my arm was not broken.

When I returned to the village, Feodor Kulikov tried to teach me how to handle a tractor. I had been assigned to the tractor brigade (see Glossary — brigade). Feodor helped me until dinnertime during my first day of work. After dinner Feodor was told that his draft notice had arrived and that he would have to report to Kizil immediately. It meant that I had to handle alone the "iron beast." I fell down on the steering wheel of the tractor and cried bitterly. "Fedja," I asked, "how will I run this machine without you?" Fedja patted me gently and said, "Katja, just do the best that you can." I continued to cry. Fedja then told me to pray that he and the other men who had been drafted would return to the village soon. It was years before any of the men came back from the war, and then only a few returned.

The tractor brigade worked long hours almost every day, yet we found time to have fun. For instance, when we walked home from the field late in the evening Nadja Alemanova, one of the young girls within our brigade, would find a reed and make it into a flute to play music. Although we were tired, we loved to dance to Nadja's tunes. It put us into a different mood, and we would joke and laugh. When I arrived home at around midnight, I had to milk the

family cow, boil potatoes for the family meal and do my other household duties. Early the next morning, before sunrise, I was awakened and walked to
the field to join the other tractor drivers. It was how I spent almost everyday
during the war years.

One of my household duties in the summer was tending the family kitchen
garden. We grew potatoes, carrots, cabbages, cucumbers and beets, and at
night, after having returned home from working all day, I had to water these
vegetables. It meant that I had to walk in the dark to the river for water. When
I returned I would hear the clanging of many buckets, and I knew that our
neighbors were also watering their kitchen gardens. My sisters, Tamara and
Nina, would usually help me. They would take their small buckets and water
the vegetables and remove the weeds that had sprung up around them.

My mother worked as well but not in the field. She was crippled due to an
illness and was unable to do physical labor such as plowing, planting or harvesting. She stayed home and watched over the children of the neighbor
women who did work in the fields. It was what life was like in the village at
that time; everyone worked according to their abilities.

I believe that the Soviet Union's victory over fascist Germany was due
largely to the hard work of the people in the villages. We in the villages were
forced to give to the State what we produced. The State took from us much
of our wheat, much of our meat, much of our milk, much of our wool and
much of everything else that we produced. The State gave us little in return
for our hard labor, and now it seems that the State has forgotten about us. The
State only remembers us when it needs our produce or when it needs our
young boys for military service. We give birth to our sons, we nurse them, we
raise them and we teach them, and then the State takes them from us to fight
its wars.

We experienced a better life in the years following the war, but our work-
load did not diminish substantially. I still had to work many hours almost
every day. I would wake up early in the morning before sunrise and walk to
the field and join the other members of the brigade. At harvest time the
brigade would mow the hay and arrange haystacks. We did many other jobs
because there was always a lot of work in the field. In the winter we did a variety of jobs in the stockyard.

We received both money and food for all of our work. We were given
money once a year and that was in the fall. We earned from ten to twenty
kopeks for each day of work. The number of days that each worker had
worked was calculated by the brigade leaders who kept records of them in
their notebooks. This was done by drawing behind a worker's name a short
vertical line for every day that she or he had worked. The money that we received we took to the city and with it purchased clothes and shoes. The

amount of wheat, vegetables and other produce that we received for each workday depended on the amount that the farm produced.

In the latter fifties I was given employment in the administrative building of the collective farm and then later the state farm. It was my job to keep the interior clean. In the winter I would arrive early and light the stoves to heat the rooms in the building. After that I would deliver work orders to a number of people in the village. The person who refused to work would have to come to the administrative building and explain to the administrators his or her reason for rejecting the job appointment. After the administrators went home for their midday meal, I would begin mopping the mud from the floors in the offices. When lunchtime was over, the floors were mopped and clean. It was also my job to prevent people from smoking in the building; I did not succeed in doing that.

Some of my most enjoyable times were spent in the Village Club watching a movie. My favorite movies were those about village life in Russia. I distinctly remember movies such as "The Peaceful Don River," "Cultivated Virgin Land," "Volga, Volga" and "The Matter Took Place in Penkovo." I did not like the war movies that were shown. Of course it was interesting to see the military equipment, the tanks, the fighter planes and the ships that were used during the war, but the fighting scenes upset me. Often I would not be able to sleep for hours after coming home from watching a war movie in the evening.

I have one daughter by the name of Tonya. She graduated from secondary school and went to Sibaie to attend a vocational school. She studied for three years to become a skilled plasterer. After graduating from the vocational school in 1972, she was told that she would have to work as a plasterer in a town or city designated by the State. When I was informed about this, I rushed to the hospital to get a certificate detailing an illness from which I suffered. I brought that certificate to the directors of the vocational school in Sibai and explained to them that I needed my daughter to take care of me in Izmaelovka. My pleas must have been effective because the directors permitted Tonya to come home, and shortly thereafter, Mr. Zeplatin, the director of our state farm, hired Tonya to renovate the buildings in Izmaelovka. While working in Izmaelovka Tonya found a husband. They were married in 1974.

In 1976 Tonya gave birth to my grandson Andrei. He now drives a large dump truck for the farm, which is no longer owned by the State. The farm is now a corporation. Before Andrei began working for the farm he was in the army and was stationed in Georgia (an area within the Soviet Union). I worried about him daily after I heard about Russia's terrible war in Chechnya. During that time I would often work at my spinning wheel. Many tears fell on that spinning wheel as I thought about the possibility that my grandson would be transferred to Chechnya. Andrei was scheduled to be in the service

for a year and a half, but when it was time for him to be released we received
a letter from him telling us that his military service had been extended by six
months because there were not enough recruits to take the place of those who
had already completed their time of service. Andrei was not sent to Chechnya, and I thank God that he returned home in good health.

There are three of us in Izmaelovka who are beyond the age of eighty, and
each of us receives a pension. The pension was determined by the number of
years that we worked on the collective and state farms. I receive 250,000
rubles each month, but since the ruble has lost much of its value over the past
several years I am not able to buy all the necessities with my pension money.
[Two hundred and fifty thousand rubles will buy ten kilograms of bread, five
kilograms of meat, three kilograms of vegetable oil, three kilograms of noodles and ten packs of cigarettes.] When the farm became a corporation each
of us who lived here received a share of the farm. As a result, I now own
twelve hectares (27 acres) of land. My land is being used by the directors of
the farm, and for the use of my land they pay me a monthly income. I am paid
with food that is produced on the farm. Every month I receive some wheat
flour, five kilograms of bread, five liters of milk and some sugar. The directors also give me special coupons with which I am able to purchase food from
the village store. I have enough to eat and have no complaints except that I
am in poor health.

I feel a constant pain in my side due to a fall down some slippery steps. My
daughter was nearby when I fell, and I cried out to her. Tonya ran to me and
tried to pick me up, but I was already as "lifeless as a whip." Now my side is
sick, and my elbow does not work well. My eyes can hardly see, but whenever I wear eyeglasses I feel pain in my eyes. I asked the doctor why my feet
can hardly walk, and he answered, "Your heart can hardly beat." I am eighty-
one years old. I think I am just too old.

I believe that God keeps me alive for several purposes and probably the
main one is to continue preparing the dead in the village for burials. To this
date I have washed and prepared thirteen people for burials. It has become a
tradition in Izmaelovka that whenever somebody dies the relatives of the deceased ask me to wash the body and prepare it. (According to Russian Orthodox tradition, relatives of the deceased are not to wash the body of the person
who has died. The washing is to be done preferably by a friend of the family).

The body of the deceased person must be prepared within two hours following death. It means that I might be called at any time of the day or night,
and I always come when I am called. After I arrive at the house of the deceased person, I begin preparing one of the rooms for the washing of the
body. I place a sheet on the floor of the room, set a chair on top of the sheet
and, with the help of the deceased person's relatives, place the naked corpse

Katherine Plotnikova (Babakatja) is seated on her bed and using a small spinning wheel to spin wool. She is wearing felt boots to keep warm.

in the chair, which has also been covered with a sheet. Meanwhile some water is being warmed on the stove, and when it is the correct temperature I will use it to wash the dead body, which is being held upright by the relatives. The body is washed twice and then dried with a towel. After that the body is dressed with the person's best clothes; they will serve as burial clothes. The body is then lifted and laid on some long wooden boards that have been placed across two chairs within the room. The boards are padded with a blanket that is covered with a clean sheet. The feet and the hands of the deceased are then bound with ribbons of calico, a candle is placed in the right hand, a cross is placed around the person's neck and an icon is laid on the chest. The body will remain in this position within the house until a coffin is prepared.

It is the responsibility of the relatives to have a coffin made and a burial place prepared. They must report the death of their family member to the administrators who will make sure that a grave is dug. They must also get a carpenter to prepare a wooden coffin. During Soviet times all of this was done free, but today the relatives must pay to have a grave dug and a coffin built.

After the grave is dug the body is buried. Before the body is placed in the coffin the calico ribbons binding the feet and the hands are removed. The icon is removed from the chest; icons are not to be put in a grave. The cross around the neck will be buried with the body.

Following the burial, the relatives will have a commemorative feast in honor of the dead family member. The sheets covering the mirrors within the house of the deceased will now be removed. The mirrors were covered immediately after the relative died. They will again be covered during the commemorative feast that the family will have on the fortieth day following the person's death. Commemorative feasts will also be held six months later and a year later. The family may have a commemorative feast every year, and traditionally the invited guests are to receive a kerchief or handkerchief.

I do not know what the future for me holds. "When I go to bed at night I think maybe I will wake up in the morning. Who knows?"

Chapter Two

"Tractor Driver"

Klavdia Vidvina (Babaklava)

Klavdia is a Cossack whose ancestors settled in the Ural Mountain region during the eighteenth century. Her grandparents were born in Izmaelovka and would experience the Great Hunger that struck Siberia in 1921. She was told about the famine and its devastating effects by her mother. Collectivization was enforced when Klavdia was a little girl, and she remembers her parents' decision to join the collective farm and the anti-religious campaign that was instituted at the time of collectivization. Her most vivid recollections are of her activities during the Great Patriotic War (see Glossary—Great Patriotic War).

During the war Klavdia was assigned by the farm authorities to work as a tractor driver. Almost all of the men in Izmaelovka were drafted into military service by the government, and the plowing, planting and harvesting were done by the women on the farm. The women worked from before sunrise till after sunset and were often hungry as they worked. At harvest time they would try to satisfy their hunger by taking some of the wheat that they harvested and eating the kernels as they worked. Following the harvest season Klavdia was sent by the collective farm authorities to the regional Machine Tractor Station. Here she along with other young women from other villages in the region would spend the winter months dismantling, cleaning, repairing and reassembling the tractors at the station. In the spring the tractors were returned to the collective farms in time for the planting season.

KLAVDIA'S ACCOUNT

I am a Cossack and my ancestors came to the Ural region of Siberia many years ago. These ancestors helped the troops of Catherine the Great defeat Yemelyan Pugachev, the leader of a peasants' war (1773–1775) against the tsarina's government. Pugachev and his forces passed through this region and established a military camp near the present location of Izmaelovka. Because my ancestors took part in the fight against Pugachev's rebellion, they were rewarded with lands near the Ural River (see Glossary—Pugachev, Yemelyan).

My mother's name was Varvava Jakovlevna Alemanova, and father's name was Andrei Afanasievich Fedotov. Mother was born in 1883, and father was born a year later. I suppose they were married to each other in 1902 because my oldest sister was born in 1903. They had many children; nine of them died and most of them died before the age of five. Many children in the village died. They died from scarlet fever, measles, smallpox and other diseases but not from hunger because there was no shortage of food in the village.

My mother often talked about the Great Hunger that struck Siberia in 1921. She said that every day refugees from the Volga River region walked along the road that passed the village. These were Russians, not Turks, and the village people called them "Samaratans" because they came from Samara located near the Volga. The refugees could hardly walk because of hunger, and many collapsed and were unable to stand up again. They died where they had fallen. Sometimes refugees would come into the village for something to eat or drink. Most of them could hardly speak, and several fell and died on the porches of the houses they approached. These people as well as those who had died on the road had to be buried, and the village leaders organized work details to bury the dead. Every day one family was assigned to look for the dead and bury them, and each family within the village was to take their turn. The bodies of the dead refugees were buried in a large common pit.

Mother never talked about the cause or causes of the Great Hunger. I know that before 1921 Russia had a history of drought but that during the droughts the people in Siberia did not die from hunger because the peasants kept food reserves. These reserves were taken from the peasants by the Soviet government during the Civil War. I have spoken to older people who remembered the Great Hunger, and they told me that the Village Council demanded that the peasants turn over the wheat that they had set aside for emergencies. The wheat was used to feed the Red Army. Although the people suffered from these exactions, nobody in Izmaelovka died from hunger.

I was a little girl when the village was turned into a collective farm. I do not remember much about that time. I recall people who I had never seen before coming into our house and advising my parents to join the collective farm. Father wanted to join; mother did not. I suspect that mother was against it because it would mean that the family would lose ownership of one of its cows. We owned two cows, but a family within a collective farm was permitted to own only one cow. I tried to convince my mother that it would be much better to join the collective farm than to live outside of it. Finally, she relented, and later my parents would often blame me, in a teasing manner, for persuading mother to agree to join the collective. The reward for doing so, they would point out, was a life of work and nothing but work.

Following collectivization, the Soviet regime closed the village church and forbade the worship of God. There was a beautiful church in the village, and there were many beautiful icons in the church. The authorities went into the church and with axes hacked the smaller icons into pieces and then burned them. The larger icons were also broken up but the pieces were used to construct cradles and beds for the nursery of the village school. For many years the wings of angels and the faces of saints could be seen in the nursery furniture. Not all of the icons in the village were destroyed. Some older people succeeded in hiding their most precious icons, and during the early years of the Great Patriotic War these icons were hung in the "Red Corner" of the houses. The "Red Corner" of a house is the right corner of the main room. It is called the "Red Corner" because Russians traditionally have considered red the most beautiful of all the colors. The owners of the icons would keep them covered with a towel or curtain for fear that the authorities would see them and confiscate them.

We were told by the authorities that we were not to celebrate Christmas or any other religious holidays. We were, for example, not permitted to paint eggs during Easter. There were many people who did anyway, but they did it secretly. These people also prepared "paskha," a rich mixture of sweetened curds, butter and raisins, which was traditionally eaten on Easter Day. The authorities told the children attending the village school that they were not to sing Easter songs. It was a Russian Orthodox tradition for children to go as groups from house to house and sing religious songs on all religious holidays. As a reward for their singing the children would receive gifts such as small pies, buns and candy. During Easter each child was given a painted egg. These religious traditions came to an end in the village.

My mother was a believer, and she would often read to me from the Bible and tell me stories about Jesus. There was one story that I remember in detail. In the story Jesus was running away from some enemies and entered a house inhabited by a young woman who was sitting near a stove and holding a child in her arms. Jesus told her to help him by dropping the child into the fire of the stove and then taking him in her arms. The young woman obeyed. She was not afraid. She dropped the child into the fire and took Jesus into her arms. Jesus was saved. After his enemies had passed by the house, Jesus left. The woman then looked in the stove and found that her child was alive and unharmed lying in a gold cradle with a gold crown on its head. I do not know why but this story left a deep impression on my soul.

The children attending the village school were not permitted to tell biblical stories, and as a student I never mentioned that my mother owned a

Bible, religious books and icons. Later, after becoming a member of the Young Pioneers organization, I urged my mother to hide the family icons (see Glossary-Young Pioneers). I did this because it was prohibited for a Young Pioneer to own an icon. It was during the Great Hunger of 1933 that mother sold her Bible for 16 kilograms of flour. The woman who bought the Bible was deeply religious and was called by the older people in the village, "Tatiana the Saint." She was always dressed in black and wore a white shawl. Later mother regretted that she had sold the Bible, but she also realized it had been done out of necessity. Now that people are allowed to worship God again, I feel safe in telling people that I do believe in God. However, I never pray because no one has ever taught me to pray.

Izmaelovka had a saint who was also considered a prophet. He was an old man who the villagers called "Daniel the Prophet." He had read many religious books and would tell many interesting stories about Jesus Christ. Maybe it was this old man who told my mother the story of the child who was placed in the Russian stove and remained unharmed. The old man died long before fascist Germany invaded the Soviet Union. He had prophesied the war, and when the war began in 1941, the villagers remembered what he had said.

Despite the actions of the authorities, many people continued to believe in God, and many also continued to give merit to superstitions. They believed that a cat, whether it was black or some other color, crossing a person's path was an omen. It meant the person would be unlucky, and it was advisable for the person immediately to return home. If a kettle produced a whistling noise while boiling it meant that some bad event would take place in that dwelling. It was believed if a person, planning to purchase or sell an item, discovered that he or she had forgotten something, the person should return home immediately. If the person did not return home, something would go wrong with the purchase or sale. The people in the village believed that placing a horseshoe at the entrance gate of a dwelling would bring success to its inhabitants.

The village people believed that a goblin lived in every village house. They believed that if a family moved to another house it was necessary to invite the goblin to join them in their new place of residence. It was the responsibility of the oldest woman in the family to ask the goblin to follow the family's move. The people believed the goblin was a valuable family asset. It was the goblin that would make the family's cattle, sheep and other livestock reproduce and multiply. The goblin also gave notice to the family about a future trouble. In such a case the goblin would approach the owner of the house at night and press his or her chest. The visit was a token of bad things to come. It was also believed that a goblin could be approached at night for advice on certain matters. People did not know what a goblin looked like, and it was believed that humans and animals were unable to see goblins. However, in Izmaelovka there was an exception.

In the village an old man by the name of Sergei Jefremor claimed that he had seen a goblin. It happened when he was a young boy and while he was playing hide and seek with his friends. He was going to hide himself in an old bathhouse, and as he entered the bathhouse he saw a goblin. The creature was sitting in front of the unlighted stove and, using a poker, was looking for something inside it. The goblin looked like an old man. He had long disheveled hair and was completely naked. Sergei was frightened with what he saw and ran out of the bathhouse. He told his friends about the goblin, and together they entered the bathhouse but found no one inside.

I began attending the village school in 1931. I was seven years old. The school was conducted in the large house of the village priest who had been removed from the village by the authorities. His removal occurred at around the same time that the village church was closed. The house had three large rooms, and these were used as classrooms. My classmates were children of different ages. During my first year, the school had only a few educational supplies. There was only one book in the school. It was not an ABC book. It was not a copybook. I do not remember what kind of book it was, but I do remember that it was large, that it had been printed with small letters and that it contained no pictures. All the students were expected to share the book, and if they were assigned to copy words they were provided with a small board. We had neither a notebook nor paper to write on, nor did we have pens or ink. When father became aware of this, he provided me with used paper from the collective farm's administrative office. The paper had writing on one side but was blank on the other side.

In my second year, the collective farm purchased several copybooks for the school. These were Russian grammar and mathematics books. Because there were not enough books for all the students, each book was shared by two students. Science and history were two subjects that we studied when I was in fourth grade. It was also the last grade that was offered in Izmaelovka.

Those of us who went on to fifth grade were sent to Kizil to attend the school in that community. Our collective farm had purchased a house in Kizil, and this became the place of residence for the students of Izmaelovka. The house consisted of two rooms. The girls lived in one room, and the boys lived in the other room. There were some thirty students living in this house. In the girls' room five of us slept together on an iron bed and two slept on a large wooden chest. A cook lived with us as well. She would receive a supply of food from Izmaelovka and would prepare three meals a day. We ate "zatiruka" almost every day (see Glossary—zatiruka).

On some weekends we would go home to spend a day with our families. We would leave Kizil on Saturday and walk some 30 kilometers (19 miles) to Izmaelovka. We brought with us our notebooks, pencils and other possessions that we carried in sacks made of cloth. We usually arrived in Izmaelovka toward evening, then we would wash ourselves and after that we would spend the rest of the evening with our families. On Sunday, the next day, we would walk back to Kizil.

In 1937 my father was arrested by the NKVD. Agents of the NKVD arrived at our home and handed my father a warrant for his arrest. He could not read the document because he was already an old man, and the small lamp in our dark living room did not give off enough light. The men took the warrant and read to my father its contents. They ordered him to open the family chests; we had two large chests. He opened one chest, which contained three rolls of bread, and then he opened the second chest in which we stored our under garments. "Where is your wealth?" they asked. My father pointed to my mother and said that she was his treasure. My mother was sick at the time and was lying on our warm Russian stove within the room. The NKVD then took my father, and I would never see him again.

I do not know why the NKVD arrested my father. We had so few possessions. Father was a regular worker on the collective farm; he was a storekeeper. Of course he was not the only one who was arrested in the village. On the same night that father was arrested, five other men were taken. Each of these men was denounced as an "enemy of the people," but what was the reason behind the denunciation? Nobody knew the answer to that question.

After Stalin's period of repressions had ended, representatives of the NKVD arrived from Chelyabinsk to investigate the arrests of my father and the five other men. They claimed that the warrants for arrest had accused the six men of burning seven large hills of straw and a storage room full of seeds. These acts of destruction never happened because if such crimes had been committed I and others my age would have remembered the huge and terrible straw fires. Some of the people who drafted the warrants of arrest are still alive, but no action will be taken against them (see Glossary - Great Purge).

After my father was arrested, I was regarded as a daughter of an "enemy of the people." The people of the village continued to greet me, but I could tell that many did not want to demonstrate a behavior that could be interpreted as sympathetic. My friends, however, continued to treat me as their friend. One very close friend was Anna Belagurina. She was the daughter of a former Red guerrilla fighter. We remained close and are friends to this day.

I stopped attending school but not because I was excluded. I left school to work to earn bread for mother and myself. If my father had not been arrested or if I had an older brother, I could have continued my studies. At that time I was interested in medicine. It was my dream to become an assistant to a doctor. When my father was arrested, the dream died. I was thirteen years old.

I was hired by the collective farm along with other girls my age to clean seeds of wheat. It was done without the use of machines. Each of us was expected to clean 38 large pails of seeds a day, and each pail contained almost 40 kilograms of seeds. It was difficult and hard work. Nobody checked our work; they must have trusted us, and we lived up to that trust because we never put in the storage room a tray of seeds that had not been cleaned properly. Cleaning seeds was my job during the winter months.

In the summer I worked as a nurse in the village nursery school. I had to take care of the babies and young children. At mealtime I would bring the babies to their mothers who worked in the stockyard or at some other place on the farm so that the mothers could breast-feed their children. The children who were older than one year would be fed by me, and I would give them milk and add to the milk a special mixture. Because the mothers of the children worked all day, I was required to be at the nursery by sunrise and would not leave until after the sun had set. There were days when mothers would not return to the village in the evening but sleep in the fields where they labored with their work brigades. On those days, I would take their children to my home for the night. Sometimes a mother would return to the village after midnight; she would then come to my home to get her child. In other cases an older brother or sister would come to the nursery to take a child home.

My job did not provide mother and me with enough food. In order to supplement our income of wheat, mother and I planted in our kitchen garden potatoes, cabbages, beets, carrots, turnips, black radishes and pumpkins. We also owned a cow, so we had enough milk, cream and curds. The law said that a family was permitted to own just one cow.

Mother supplemented the family income by working. Because she suffered from rheumatism, an illness she acquired after giving birth to her first child, mother could only work at home. She acquired raw wool and carded it, spun it into yarn and knitted the yarn into mittens, stockings and socks that were sold to the more wealthy families in the village. Izmaelovka had both rich people and poor people. The villagers who did not have the money to buy these items paid for them with eggs, meat or other foods.

When the war began, I and several other girls in Izmaelovka were selected to become tractor drivers and combine operators. I remember how I cried after the director of the machine shop on our collective farm informed me that I would be leaving the village to drive a tractor and operate a combine. My mother wept as well after I told her the bad news; she hated to see me go. The leaders of the collective farm had given me an order, and I was expected to obey it.

Verkhneuralsk had a combine operator and tractor driver school, and it was to this town that we were sent. We traveled by lorry first to Magnitogorsk, and then we took another lorry to Verkhneuralsk. Upon our arrival at the vocation school, which was simply a machine shop that had at one time been privately owned, the director checked our passes and then ordered his assistant to take us to our living quarters. It was a house with three large rooms, and I suspect that the building had been expropriated from its owner following the October Revolution (see Glossary—October Revolution). The house would become a home for one hundred girls from various areas who had been sent to Verkhneuralsk to study heavy machinery. Each room within the house was furnished with many small beds and nothing more. No cabinets were necessary since each of us had brought so little. For example, I had only a small bag in which I kept an old dress and an extra pair of socks. I had no toothbrush and no tooth powder, and I had no soap or towel. It was just as well, because the school had no bathhouse. Fortunately, the weather was warm so that we could, during our free time, go to the nearest river and swim.

Our instruction began on the day after we arrived. In the machine shop we were introduced to the type of tractor and combine we were expected to drive and operate. Our instructors were experienced teachers, but during our month of instruction all but one of the instructors disappeared. Those who disappeared had been drafted into military service and were sent to the front. The instructor who remained was an old man.

At the end of the month of our instruction each of us received a diploma. We were now licensed to drive a tractor and operate a combine, but in reality only a few of the girls knew how to drive or operate the machines. Most of us knew almost nothing about this heavy equipment.

After I returned to Izamaelovka and after I was brought to the field that was to be harvested, I broke down and cried. The chairman of the collective farm who was in the field to watch the harvest and observe the workings of the machinery came up to me and asked me why I was crying. I replied that I did not know how to operate a combine. It was a complicated machine, and I had received just one month of training. "Don't worry," he replied, "In a minute Matvey Petrovich will come and help you." Matvey was an older man who was a tractor driver. He arrived shortly, hitched his tractor to the combine and pulled me around the field for three days, but I still did not know how to operate the combine. I was replaced by a young boy, and I became his assistant.

After the harvest campaign, I was sent to the Machine Tractor Station in Obruchevka. My job was to help repair the tractors and other machines that were kept there and prepare them for the spring plowing and planting campaigns. To my surprise, I was ordered by the director of the Machine Tractor Station to become a tractor driver. I participated in a two-month tractor driver course. Upon completion of this course, I was able to repair and drive a tractor, and I was a good tractor driver.

While in Obruchevka, I lived with several other girls my age who had also been assigned to work at the Machine Tractor Station. We lived in a house that was too small for us. The house was not furnished with beds, so we slept on wide boards or on the stove. We were not given soap, and a bathhouse was not provided so within a short period of time we suffered from lice. Relief from the lice came once or twice a month when we were permitted to go home to be with our families. Upon my arrival home, I would run to the bathhouse and wash myself and my dress. I would stay in the bathhouse until my dress was dry because at that time I had nothing else to wear. I also did not have an iron with which to iron my dress so I would put the dress back on wrinkled after it was dry. Then I would spend the evening and night with my family. It felt good to be free of lice. After I returned to Obruchevka, the lice reappeared.

In time, I was assigned to the tractor brigade of Izmaelovka. The brigade consisted of fifteen young girls and several boys. The tractors were in bad condition; they needed to be repaired frequently and we were expected to repair them in the field. It was difficult for one or even two of us to remove the heavy housing that covered the tractor engine. In order to lift the metal housing we used a large block of wood as a base and placed on top of it a birch pole that we used as a lever. The tractors were made in Chelyabinsk, and each was designed with a huge flywheel that had to be turned to start the engine (see glossary-Chelyabinsk). Thinking back to this time, I do not know how I found the strength to turn the flywheel. I was just sixteen years old at the time.

One year I was told to take my tractor to the state farm named "Ural." We in Izmaelovka had finished our sowing campaign, but the workers in "Ural" had not and Gregory, another young driver in our tractor brigade, and I were told to help the people of "Ural" sow their crops. On the way to "Ural," Gregory stopped at his home and promised that he would catch up with me. After I had driven a distance, I noticed that water was coming out of my tractor pipes so I stopped the tractor in order to repair it. As I examined the pipes, a strong wind blew the lower part of my dress into the running engine. Suddenly, I felt a strong pull at my dress, and within a few seconds I was naked. The dress had been torn from my body. Fortunately, an old man happened to be standing nearby, and he gave me his old sheepskin coat. I went back to Izmaelovka, but I had no other dress at home. Most of the young girls in Izmaelovka had only one dress. What was I to do? I had nothing to wear, and I had to go back to work. When my mother came home from some errand, I told her about my dilemma. She told me not to worry; she said she would make me a skirt from large patches of rough textured canvas that she was using to make sacks. Mother sewed the skirt, and I went to "Ural" in that skirt. It was uncomfortable, but I had nothing else to wear.

As a tractor driver I was rewarded on many occasions for doing my job well. The rewards were gifts, and the gifts were usually baked scones made with wheat flour. The people in the collective farms rarely were given wheat flour for their labors. They ate a substitute, which was a powder that looked like wheat flour but was made from grasses and primarily from one grass named goosefoot; it grew among the wheat.

Workers in the field were not permitted to eat the wheat seeds that were planted, but we did anyway to survive. The authorities came to the fields many times to check up on us to determine whether or not we were stealing some of the seeds. They never caught us making "kurmatch" which is wheat seeds that have been fried in oil. Usually, I would ask the young boy whose duty it was to help me with the tractor to take some wheat seeds from the seeding machine. Then I gave him some diesel fuel, and he used that to fry the seeds in some machine oil that he placed in a bucket. After I completed a circle around the field, the "kurmatch" was ready to eat. When the seeds were fried they became carbon black, but inside they were a snow-white. They were deliciously sweet. To tell you the truth, the workers in our tractor brigade survived each sowing campaign because of "kurmatch." All day long we ate "kurmatch." As we plowed, cultivated and planted we dropped the "kurmatch" in our mouths, grain by grain.

One day our favorite Party leader from Kizil joined us in eating "kurmatch." His name was Vasili Vasilievich Skriabin, and periodically he came to Izmaelovka to examine our work. Vasili was honest and kind. Whenever he visited our brigade in the field, he would eat dinner with us. The other Party leaders would always eat a specially prepared meal at the house of the chairman of the collective farm. Vasili would work in the field with us. He would help us fill the seeding machines or do some other kind of job. On the day that we shared our "kurmatch" with Vasili he was hungry. He ate it with great pleasure. Suddenly there appeared a car with another Party representative from Kizil. Vasili knew it was a crime to eat the wheat seeds so he put the remaining "kurmatch" in his cone peaked cap and placed the cap on his head. The "kurmatch" was hot and Vasili suffered, but the other Party representative did not discover our crime. Following the incident, we considered Vasili a close friend, and we were not afraid to share with him our innermost thoughts.

The brigade worked hard and the working hours were long. Usually, we would begin our work at sunrise and would not stop working until the arrival of midnight. In spite of the long working hours we found time to laugh, sing and even dance. We would sing during our breaks and also as we walked home from the field at night. I do not remember the words of the songs that were sung, but I do remember they were popular Russian songs and folk songs. We also liked to tell each other anecdotes. These short stories were about unlucky soldiers and faithless lovers. They were never about Lenin or

Stalin or any of the Party leaders. We did not dare make fun of our political leaders for fear of being punished. We also liked to share interesting stories about ourselves. We all laughed when I told the members of the brigade about the time my dress got caught in a moving part of my tractor, and I was stripped naked.

Because we spent so much time together, we treated each other as sisters and brothers. Sometimes we would quarrel. It was usually an act of stealing that would lead to a quarrel. If I left my "kurmatch" somewhere and another member of the brigade came along and ate it I would find out who had stolen my food and confront that individual. There was always a shortage of spare machine parts. If someone took a nut or a bolt from my box of spare parts it would lead to a quarrel. Our quarrels would not last long, and they were quickly forgotten.

We had other problems that loomed much larger in our minds. There were the Communist Party officials and the rules that they enforced. Those who violated them were punished severely. One of my friends refused to work as a combine operator and, as a consequence, was imprisoned for several months and was released only after she agreed to operate a combine. If someone was late for work that person might be imprisoned for up to six months. We were constantly on our guard. We had to be careful in our conversations. We knew that we would suffer punishment from the authorities if they learned that we had expressed opinions that were unacceptable to the Communist Party.

After the war I became a member of the Komsomol. My membership was the result of a series of steps that began with my application for admission to the organization. Upon review of my application, two Komsomol members recommended me. I was given the Komsomol rules and its program of activities and told to become familiar with them. After a week or two, I was invited to a Komsomol meeting and asked several questions about the organization's rules and program and about my work within the collective farm. The interview went well, and I was placed on probation for one month as a member of the village Komsomol. After this, its leader and I traveled to Kizil to meet with the Regional Komsomol Committee. It was customary for this committee to examine the competence of a newly invited member. They also checked the person's knowledge of the organization's history and its rules. If the person was unable to answer satisfactorily the questions, she or he was given another opportunity to do so within several days. The procedure in Kizil took no more than fifteen minutes, and my invitation was approved (see Glossary—Komsomol).

In time, I was elected by the other members of the village Komsomol to be the leader of the organization. Back in 1938, I did not dream that this would ever happen to me. At that time I was viewed as the daughter of an "enemy of the people." Time had passed, and I had worked hard for the collective farm during the war years. Through my work I had gained a new identity. Now I was not only a member of the village Komsomol but its leader.

As members of the Komsomol we would go into the fields and read the regional newspapers to the workers during their break. The newspapers informed the readers about the work accomplishments of the collective farms within the region and about certain workers who exceeded their work requirements. The names of slackers were also printed. The workers in the fields listened attentively.

The village Komsomol had its own newspaper called "Fighting Sheets." In "Fighting Sheets" we would criticize the workers in the collective farm who we believed to be slackers. These were people who often failed to come to work or would arrive at their work station late. If a caretaker of the farm's pigs did not tend to the pigs properly and the pig pens were not cleaned, we would report that in "Fighting Sheets." If a brigade leader treated his workers badly, we would report that. In response to our reports, the accused would improve their work performance and their behavior. Having done that, they would then deny the accusations that we had brought against them in our newspaper. They would do this to save face for they were concerned about their reputation within the village, but almost everyone knew that what we had reported was true. It gave us a feeling of accomplishment; we believed that through our "Fighting Sheets" we had contributed to the improvement of the collective farm.

The Komsomol meetings were held in the Village Club building. The building was representative of most buildings used for administrative purposes in the collective farm. Hanging on the inside walls of these buildings were portraits of Marx, Engles, Lenin and Stalin. These portraits were taken from magazines and placed in picture frames. It was also possible to purchase a portrait of one of these men on an inexpensive postcard at the local post office. The people of the village would hang these in their homes alongside the photographs of grandparents and other family members. Unfortunately, I have no photographs of my ancestors.

The village library was housed in the Village Club building. Here the villagers could come to read newspapers and magazines. People were permitted to check out books and bring them home, but few adults did that. Most adults had no time to read. I loved to read and would take home from the village library books that interested me. I remember reading "The Holder of the Golden Star," "The White Birch" and "Two captains." I also read the works of the great Russian authors such as Alexander Pushkin and Leo Tolstoy. I did not read the works of Theodor Dostoyevsky; his writings are much too difficult to understand.

I was introduced to my husband after the war. My husband was not a native of Izmaelovka; he was born in Karagaika. All of the younger men of Izmaelovka had been drafted into military service during the war, and only a few returned home after the war. My husband and I were married in 1949. There was neither a wedding celebration nor a wedding feast because our families had no money to arrange them. It still makes me sad because a wedding celebration and a wedding feast are two important events in a woman's life. It was a bad beginning to a marriage that was less than desirable.

In the village if two young people decided to become husband and wife there were several traditional procedures that were carried out before the wedding ceremony. The procedures began with an announcement made by the future bridegroom's parents to their relatives that their son intended to get married. Then the relatives chose two people, a male and female, to go to the future bride's family to decide upon a wedding date with the bride's parents. It was just a formality because the date of the wedding had already been set by the marriage couple. After the wedding date was agreed upon by both families, a period of so-called "evenings" began. Friends of the bride and bridegroom would gather at the home of the bride's parents every evening up to the day of the wedding to sing songs, dance and just have a good time together.

On the day of the wedding, the bride and bridegroom would go to the Village Council to be registered as a new family. (Before collectivization a couple would be married in the village church). The bridegroom was to go and get his bride with a beautiful cart pulled by horses. Meanwhile, the bride and her girl friends would wait for him. When the bridegroom arrived at the house of the bride's parents it was traditional for him to "buy" his wife. He did that with the assistance of a friend. The friend would enter the main room of the house and approach a table surrounded by children who were related to the bride and drop some coins on the table. The children would grab the money and demand still more. The bridegroom's friend would then yell at the children and strike the table with his whip. The children would scatter, but all of this was done in fun. Then the bridegroom would enter the room and buy a flower named "krasotka" (the beauty) and his bride. He would usually pay the amount that the bride's girl friends demanded, and the girl friends were expected to demand an acceptable amount. Then the bridegroom would take his bride in the beautiful cart to the Village Council to be registered or married.

After the marriage was registered at the Village Council, the newly married couple would participate in several days of feasting. The bridegroom would take his bride to his parents' home where his relatives had already prepared a feast. The bridegroom was expected to carry his bride in his arms into the house. They would then sit at the head of the prepared table; their fathers would sit next to them on each side, and the mothers would sit next to the fathers. Other close relatives would also sit at the head table. Before the food was served, all the guests were given a small glass of vodka. After drinking this down, they were given a second. After they drank their second glass of vodka, homemade cheese was served. Then a female relative of the bridegroom would take the handle of a frying pan and pretend that she was drawing on the ceiling while shouting, "a cow has a heifer and a sow has a suckling-pig." The father of the bridegroom would respond to all of this by giving his gifts to the married couple. The father of the bride would then announce his gifts and so would the other relatives. After this, the feast would begin in earnest. The food included different pies, buns, fried fish, boiled chickens, stewed meat, boiled potatoes and other dishes. There would be much to drink as well, and often the guests drank too much. The bride and bridegroom were not to drink on this first day of feasting. They were supposed to leave the party and go to the house in which they would spend their first night as husband and wife.

On the following morning, the married couple would be awakened by the wedding guests and brought to the home of the bride's parents where they were to eat a breakfast of pancakes. It marked the beginning of the second day of feasts. I remember this feast clearly because I witnessed it on several occasions as a little girl. The guests would not only eat pancakes but they would also drink a large quantity of vodka. The wedding guests would remain all day and into the evening at the home of the bride's parents.

The next day, the wedding guests went to the home of the bridegroom's parents to extinguish a fire that the bridegroom had lighted on the day of the wedding. It started the third day of feasts. Throughout this day the guests ate and drank vodka. They sang and danced to the accompaniment of an accordion. Many humorous stories were told. The young women and girls would dress up in smocks to look like doctors or as devils from hell and walk along the village streets. Toward the evening everyone returned to their homes. The three days of feasting were over.

During the first years of marriage my husband and I were poor due to the high taxes that were placed upon us by the State. We were required to provide the State with milk and eggs. A family that owned a cow, pig or sheep was required to give the State 30 kilograms of meat annually. The State demanded from each family annually a certain amount of wool. The families that did not own sheep would have to buy the wool and then give that wool to the State. The taxes kept us poor. We received wheat for our workdays but not enough. We were constantly preoccupied with obtaining food.

In the early 1960s I would make my own bread. The village store did not sell bread. Two major ingredients, wheat flour and hops, were needed to make bread. The wheat flour was acquired from the collective farm through my labor. The hops, which grew along the Ural River, I received from my relative in Kizil. A large sack of hops would last me three years. The hops would be mixed with the wheat flour to make leavened dough. I would do this in the evening, and then throughout the night I would wake up several times to mix and pound the dough again. Early the next morning I would light my stove, and when the temperature in the oven was right I would, using a long wooden paddle, place six round lumps of dough on the clay floor of the oven. It was possible to bake six large rolls of bread at the same time. It took about two hours to bake the bread, and during that time I would have the window of the kitchen open so that anyone who passed by our house would experience the aroma of bread baking. Bread that is baked in a Russian stove is indescribably delicious. The bread that I buy now in our village store is soft and white and it looks pretty, but it has little flavor.

Like most other families in the village, we owned some livestock and had a kitchen garden. We kept our sheep, cow, pig and fowl in the yard around our house. Our kitchen garden was a small piece of land near the river that flowed along the outskirts of the village. Having it near the river made watering the plants easy, and every year we would plant potatoes, carrots, cabbages, beetroots, cucumbers, tomatoes and pumpkins.

Medical care was available, and the village had its own doctor and a small hospital. For instance, if my daughter suffered from a toothache she would be taken to the doctor, and he would pull out the tooth. If she suffered a terrible headache the doctor would give her pills free of charge. The person who contracted malaria would be treated with quinine, but he or she was expected to continue working. If someone was unable to walk because of a fever, the doctor would admit that person to the village hospital and submit to the farm authorities a certificate describing the person's illness. The certificate was designed to protect the ailing worker; his or her absence from work was now justified. The certificate would also help the authorities with their record keeping. A worker was not to be paid for days that he or she had not worked. I do not know if anyone in the village was prescribed eyeglasses. I remember only one person who used eyeglasses; it was an old man who worked as an accountant.

I myself worked as an accountant. Upon my release from tractor driving, I was assigned to keep records for a field brigade and later at the village threshing floor. After that I worked as a record keeper for the collective farm's cattle breeding brigade. Shortly after Izmaelovka became a state farm, I began to study, through a correspondence study program, to be an accountant. After finishing my studies, I worked as an accountant for some fourteen years until I retired. An accountant has important responsibilities and must be honest.

Being assigned to that position probably indicates that the authorities had forgotten that I was the daughter of a former "enemy of the people." It might also mean that through my performance at my previous jobs I had proven that I was worthy of their trust.

In the 1960s life in the village improved dramatically. The improvement came after our collective farm became a state farm in 1964. The State began to support us. Taxes were reduced, and workers were paid a monthly salary. The people worked hard and long hours, but their efforts were rewarded. Socialist competitions were organized, and on Soviet holidays the leading workers in the village were recognized and honored. Their large portraits were placed along the "Avenue of Honor" within the village, and there they were to remain for an entire year. Unfortunately, this tradition has died.

"Sabbotuniks" were organized to improve the appearance of the collective farm. A "sabbotunik" was a Saturday that was designated as a workday. On this day the people who worked for the farm would go to their job sites and make some noticeable improvements. If a woman worked at the village store she might sweep the sidewalk in front of the building, she might pick up the trash around the store and she might wash the floor inside the store. The men who worked at the stockyard might repair some fences or re-hang a gate that had been removed from its hinges. No one was paid for the work that was done on this day. The idea behind a "sabbotunik" was that everyone donated a day of work for the improvement of the farm.

During the Brezhnev years we enjoyed good harvests and many products could be found on the shelves in the village store. There were salamis, jams and candies. We were able to purchase sausages, different kinds of fish, cereals and many other foods. If the village store did not have certain products, the people would go to Sibai or Magnitogorsk to purchase the items in the stores there. At that time it was possible to travel to Magnitogorsk by car because there were several people in the village who owned cars. Firsonovich was the first to buy a car. Then Korsakov and after that Kriukov purchased cars. These men were leading workers.

Life today is much worse than it was during the Brezhnev years. I receive my pension money every month, but after I pay for electricity, water and heating I have enough money to buy only bread, noodles, cereals and vegetable oil. I cannot afford to buy candies or salami. My son visited me recently and opened up my kitchen cupboard in search of something to eat. "Oh, mother," he muttered sadly, "I remember the days when your cupboard was always full of delicious things to eat. You had candies, jams, honey cakes and other baked goods. The cupboard is empty now."

I do not mind being poor as long as God gives me good health. I do not desire anything more. Unfortunately, most of the village people of my generation have lost their good health; they probably lost it due to the war. During our last Victory Day celebration only eleven people came to the gathering. I remember a time when one hundred and fifty people attended the celebration (see Glossary — Victory Day).

I have already made preparations for my death and funeral. In the 1960s I began setting aside a small percentage of my monthly income for my funeral. I placed the money in the state bank. Today the figure of my savings is quite large, but because of high inflation over the last several years the figure means nothing. The money has lost its value, and I wonder who will pay for my funeral. My children paid for their father's funeral, but who will pay for mine?

Chapter Three

"Dedicated Nurse"

Juliana Selezneva

Juliana was drafted into the military as a nurse shortly after the Soviet Union was invaded in 1941. She was required to report to the community of Kizil immediately and from there she was brought to Magnitogorsk and then to Chelyabinsk, which had a large railway station on the Trans Siberian Railroad. From there Juliana and eighteen other nurses were transported to the Far East. After arriving at their destination, they nursed the wounded soldiers who were brought to their facility from various military fronts.

It was while Juliana was a military nurse that she met her husband. Both were released from the army for medical reasons. Upon their release they were assigned to work as physician and midwife in Izmaelovka. They were also responsible for the medical care of the inhabitants in three nearby villages. Whenever there was a medical emergency in another village, during the day or during the night, Juliana and her husband were brought to the village by horse and cart.

JULIANA'S ACCOUNT

I was born in 1921 in a village named Kazbakh. The village is located in the Kizil region. My parents told me that the year of my birth was a time of great hunger, and they and the others in the village suffered terribly.

Seven years later Kazbakh was turned into a collective farm. Representatives of a newly formed Village Council went to the wealthy families in the village and ordered them to vacate their houses. These Kulaks were then brought to a railway station in carts that were pulled by horses. I remember seeing them leave. Each family had some extra clothes, a few linens, some dishes and of course a samovar. The men tried to appear optimistic, but their wives broke down and wept. Their horses and their other livestock as well as their other possessions, which they were forced to leave behind, became the property of the collective farm. Those of us who remained in the village learned that the evicted families had been taken to eastern Siberia.

My father was one of the first men in the village to join the collective farm. He believed strongly in socialism and had fought in the Red Army during the Civil War. He, my mother and I lived with my mother's stepfather who owned two horses, several cows and many sheep. All of these animals except for one cow and a sheep were taken from him and became property of the collective farm. The confiscation of his animals made him angry, and sometimes he would express his anger toward my father. He said that if my father should ever suffer from economic hardship he had only himself to blame.

During collectivization the village church was turned into a storage building. This was done after the sudden disappearance of the village priest, an older man who was hard of hearing. The church, which was surrounded by lilac bushes, was a beautiful structure with five crosses. The four small crosses were removed quite easily, but the removal of the large cross that was mounted on the church dome proved to be difficult. A rope was tied to the cross, and a tractor was used to pull at it. The cross did not budge. Finally, the entire dome was sawed off. As it was pulled off the roof, the top of the cross pierced the ground. It went so deep into the ground that it took hours to remove it. The large bell of the church was also removed, but the small one remained untouched so that it could be used to alarm the village people about a fire or a snowstorm. The large bell and the crosses were brought to Magnitogorsk, and there they were melted down. The church icons were also removed from the building, and they were burned. Having stripped the church of its religious ornamentations the authorities wanted to turn it into a village club, but the people were opposed to that. They felt that it was sacrilegious to have dances in the former house of God. The building was used eventually as a storage place for seed. It's a shame that the church was not preserved as a historical monument.

The year of collectivization was also the year that I began attending school, but within a year the village school, a wooden building, was destroyed by a fire. Thereafter, school was conducted, for a while, in several empty houses that had belonged to the Kulaks who had been removed from the village during collectivization. Each of these houses was used by two groups of students. One group would meet in the morning, and the other group would meet in the afternoon.

After I finished school in 1935, I began working as an attendant at a state hospital. I took the job after I was told by the leaders at Kazbakh that I was too young to work on the collective farm. The state hospital was located in a state farm named "The Way of October." While working as an attendant I took courses in nursing, and on the completion of these courses I became a nurse.

My responsibilities as a nurse varied. I was to light the stoves in the hospital each morning and find the time during the day to wash the floors of the building. I was required to be on duty for a period of twenty-four hours and then was given a forty-eight hour break. While on duty I was to tend to the cares of the patients. I was required to give them their medicines at the appointed times, to give them injections and to check their temperatures. The hospital did not have special medical equipment so physical therapy was not administered and cardiograms and x-rays were not taken. If a patient needed the kind of care that the hospital was not able to provide, the patient was brought to a larger hospital in Magnitogorsk or in a city such as Troitzk.

In 1937 I began taking courses in pharmacy. At the same time I worked in the pharmacy office of the state hospital. A doctor's assistant would give me a patient's prescription, and I would prepare it with liquids or powders that were stored in large jars. There were no pills at that time. All the ingredients in a prescription had to be weighed, mixed and then packaged. If the prescription came in the form of a powder, I would put it in a paper package and give it to the patient when he or she came to pick it up.

I left the state hospital in 1939 to attend a medical vocation school in Magnitogorsk. I was assigned to a three-year program of study and completed the course work in two years. Upon the completion of my studies, I was notified that the Soviet military needed my services; I was to be drafted into the army. It was July 1941.

I was living with my mother and sister in Kazbakh when I received my orders to go to war. My mother started to cry, but I was in too much of a hurry to comfort her. A man with a cart drawn by two horses had already arrived at the house to bring me and others in the village to Kizil. It was evening, and we traveled all night to arrive in Kizil early the next morning. At the Kizil recruiting station my long beautiful hair was cut. Thereafter, we were placed on trucks and brought to the train station in Magnitogorsk. From Magnitogorsk we were brought to Chelyabinsk.

In Chelyabinsk I became one of eighteen young nurses who were sent as a group to the Far East. The trip would take twelve days in a train that had been used to haul livestock before the war. Our enclosed car was hot and dimly lit. Fresh air and sunlight entered only through four small square openings located just below the roofline of the car. Straw had been spread across the floor, and on that we sat and slept. During the day we would sing songs to entertain ourselves. We also shared the food that we had brought from home; we had with us bread, boiled eggs and scones. Sometimes, when the train stopped at a community railway station, the engineer would come to our car to ask us how we were doing. At a station we would try to buy more food from the local citizens who had come to the station to sell produce from their gardens. We also used the station's toilet facilities. As we traveled farther and farther east we passed through fewer and fewer communities. Nevertheless, the train was stopped at certain time intervals so that we could relieve ourselves either behind some bushes or out in the open. It was toward the end of the trip that large groups of soldiers who were riding in the other cars got off the train to join their military divisions.

Finally, we arrived at the Dauriya station situated near the Manchurian border. Dauriya was our destination. As we jumped out of our car, we saw only a small village that was surrounded by hills. In Dauriya we were each given a military uniform with a high collared tunic, a field service cap bearing a red star, pultees to wrap around our ankles and calves, boots and an overcoat. There were no military skirts in the unit's storage so we made our own out of rolls of dark blue fabric. The skirts looked great.

Our first project was to set up a hospital. We found a one-story building that had been used as a barracks for soldiers before the war and converted that into a hospital. We had plenty of beds. We arranged one room for surgical procedures and another room for minor procedures. We had surgical tools and boxes of sterilization but no patients. For two years not one injured soldier was brought to Dauriya for medical treatment.

In Dauriya the military officers would give the hospital workers lessons in politics. They tried to explain to us why fascist Germany had invaded the Soviet Union. They said that our country was the first in the world in which a valid Communist society was being constructed. We all believed that Communism would provide everyone with a better life. However, if you had asked me to explain Communism, as a philosophy, I would not have been able to do so. I only knew that before the war life in Soviet Russia became better and better, and I liked it.

The hospital staff was moved west after the Soviet Union signed a non-aggression pact with the Japanese in Manchuria in 1943. We were moved to a place near Lake Baikal. Here there arrived soldiers from the western front. Many of the wounded had lost their arms or legs or both. Many suffered from first, second or third degree burns. Many needed blood, and I and the other nurses would offer to donate our own blood.

Our work schedule was twelve hours a day every other day. A workday was filled with checking on the patients. The patients were given the recommended medicines, and those who couldn't walk were brought their meals. The food at the hospital was rather good. The patients were always served lots of fish, either fried or boiled in soups. They were also fed vegetable soup, gruel, noodles and potatoes. Caring for the sick and wounded was hard work, and there was little time for idle chatter when I was on duty. On my days off, I would write down the events of the previous days in a diary. After a while I was told that information about my military division and its location and its commanders was not to be recorded. I stopped keeping a diary.

It was in the military that I met Alexandr Seleznev who became my husband. Alexandr was a lieutenant and a doctor's assistant. Being an officer he was given the keys to the cabinet in which the hospital's drugs were stored. One day he gave the keys to one of the nurses, and she got into the cabinet to steal drugs for her own consumption. Her theft was discovered after an officer found her fast asleep; apparently the drugs had induced sleep. Because Alexandr had given her the keys to the drug cabinet, he was ordered to remain confined to his quarters as punishment.

On the night of the day of the discovered theft, Alexandr left his quarters to come to the hospital. I was on duty at the time along with another nurse. When Alexandr saw me he began talking to us and telling interesting stories, but while he was with us another officer discovered that Alexandr had left his quarters without permission. The officer reported Alexandr's disappearance to the hospital commander. Once again Alexandr was apprehended and brought before the commander. To avoid more severe discipline, Alexandr told the commander that his absence could be explained. He said that while he was gone he had married me. The commander found Alexandr's explanation incredible so he ordered that I be summoned to confirm Alexandr's story. Alexandr, realizing that he was in a predicament, asked the commander not to invite me into his office because he said I was a shy girl and would be offended if I was asked to verify before the commander our marriage. The commander agreed but ordered that Alexandr should, as soon as possible, get our marriage registered officially by the local Village Council.

The next day Alexandr informed me about the commander's order. I was in shock. Alexandr had lied to the commander. I told him I would not go to the Village Council because I hardly knew him, and all this was unexpected. Alexandr would not give up and eventually persuaded me to be his wife. On that same day our marriage was registered at the local Village Council. Of course we didn't have a wedding feast, but we were given our own room.

Shortly after we were married we were released from the military for medical reasons. Alexandr was suffering from an aggravated stomach ulcer. It was a condition that he had incurred before the war as a student in the medical vocation school in Novosibirsk. I was also ill. My body had become weak physically because of the many times that I had given blood for the patients' blood transfusions.

Upon our release from the military, Alexandr and I traveled to Kazbakh to visit my relatives. We planned to stay in Kazbakh for a short while and then move to Novokuznetsk, a small coal-producing town where Alexandr had worked before he was drafted into the army. Our plans were altered after we left Kazbakh. First, we traveled to Kizil to acquire from the recruiting office located there the necessary passes which would allow us to travel to Novokuznetsk. These passes were required during the war years. The officials in Kizil would not give us the passes; they told us that medical personnel were needed in the Kizil region. They then sent us to the Regional Executive Committee, and they in turn appointed us to work as physician and midwife in Izmaelovka.

We moved to Izmaelovka, but Alexandr was required to provide medical treatment to the ill in three other villages as well. These villages were Michaelovka, Zdanovka and Kondurovka and each was located in the Kizil region. If any person in one of these villages should need Alexandr's assistance a man with a horse and cart would arrive in Izmaelovka to bring my husband to the person in need. Sometimes two carts from different villages arrived at the same time. Usually, Alexandr would be gone for several hours when he assisted a patient in another village, and after he returned he would tell me about the patient's condition.

The patients in Izmaelovka were treated in our home. We were provided with a three-room house, and one of the rooms was used by my husband as an office and a medical examination room. It was furnished with a table, a couch for the patients, a large medicine cabinet and a stove. There was only one entrance to the house, and that was the entrance to our living quarters. Thus, when a patient arrived the person was brought through our home and then into my husband's office.

I began assisting Alexandr in 1944 after I gave birth to our first child. Whenever my husband was called to come to another village, I would go with him. We traveled almost everyday, and sometimes we traveled at night. We had so many cases that we took no vacations. We tried our best to do what we could for each patient. Although my husband was not a trained dentist, there were times when he would have to extract a tooth. Sometimes he would administer therapy, and sometimes he would perform surgery. The most common sickness at that time was an ordinary cold, and the remedy for that illness was simply an aspirin.

Alexandr joined the Communist Party in Izmaelovka and was eventually elected its leader. The position provided him no privileges, but it did give him additional work. He asked me to join him as a Party member. He even brought home an application for admission for me to complete. As I began to fill it out, he told me to stop. When I asked him why, he said that being a member of the Party involved a lot of work, and he felt that having one family member in the Party was enough. I accepted my husband's decision because I considered him to be the head of our family. If he had changed his mind and told me to apply for Party membership, I would have done that.

I remember Victory Day, May 9, 1945. I was sitting near our house with our baby daughter when it was announced over the radio that the war was over. All the people in Izmaelovka were happy. They laughed and danced with joy.

Following the war my husband was provided with penicillin. It was a new drug that could be used as an antibiotic for many illnesses. Once my husband rode a bicycle from Michaelovka to Izmaelovka, and during the ride it rained and he became ill with pneumonia. He treated himself with penicillin and that saved him. I remember a tractor driver from Zdanovka and a worker in Izmaelovka contracting measles, a children's illness. Both were given penicillin; both recovered from the illness.

The medicines that Alexandr used were provided to him by the medical center in Kizil. The patients paid my husband for the medicines with which he treated them, and the money was sent to Kizil. If a person suffered an accident on the job working for the collective farm then the first aid that was administered and the medicines that were given to the patient were paid by the Village Council.

Accidents were common in the villages. Once there was a terrible fire in Kondurovka. It happened when a woman was about to light the stove in her bathhouse. She poured some kerosene from her lamp onto the logs in the stove. Suddenly, a blast of fire emerged through the stove opening. It surprised the woman so much that she dropped her lamp causing kerosene to pour over the floor. Immediately, the woman and her daughter were engulfed by fire. I was informed about the accident and traveled directly to Kondurovka. When I arrived there was nothing I could do to treat the mother and daughter. Instead, I had them brought to the hospital in Kizil. The following day, both of them died from severe burns.

The birth rate following the war increased considerably and with it the demand for midwives. I would often be called to assist a woman who was about to give birth. Sometimes a woman would be in labor for many hours. Many of the women would pray to God to help them through their labor, and after their children were delivered they would thank God for his gift to them. These were wonderful moments, and I would join the women in prayer. I prayed because I believed in God, and I continue to believe in God. My faith in God goes back to when I was a child. My father was a leader in the village church, and he would often take me to church.

I was requested many times by pregnant women to help them abort their babies. Aborting a child was a criminal offense for both the mother and the person who assisted her. I would tell the women who requested an abortion to go and seek medical help at the hospital in Kizil. Many of the women instead went to older women who would agree to help them. I was told that one of these women was Anna Alemanova. She, I was told, would use a catheter to abort an unborn child. Some abortions would cause the mothers to suffer from excessive bleeding and infection. Whenever that happened, Alexandr and I would be called upon to assist the bleeding women. If we asked the women about their condition and what had caused it, they would never tell us the truth.

I now live with my sister in a two-room apartment. We each receive a pension, but the money is not enough to buy food and clothes. We could get some land for a kitchen garden, but the plot of land would be outside of the village proper and that does us no good. It would be difficult to take care of it that far away. People will also steal from a kitchen garden if it is not located near the owner's place of residence. I could also have a cow, but I would have to keep it in the village stockyard. It would mean that I would have to walk to the stockyard three times a day. I am not able to do that. My four children are aware of my predicament, and on my birthday each of them send me money that I use to buy clothes.

All of my children have become professionals. My oldest son studied in the medical university in Chelyabinsk. He is a doctor and lives with his wife and two daughters in Tolyatti, a city along the Volga River. My two daughters graduated from the pedagogical university in Magnitogorsk. One continues to live and teach there. The other worked for a while as a teacher in Izmaelovka, and then she moved to the Orenburg region to become the principal of a school. My youngest son graduated from Chelyabinsk Medical University and now works in Chelyabinsk as a physician.

Chapter Four

"Milk Maid"

Maria Murzina Grigorievna

Maria was raised in a turbulent household. Her father was a handsome man who could play the hand accordion, the most popular musical instrument in the villages of Siberia. Women were attracted to him, and he was attracted to them and became involved in extra marital relations. He also drank too much and would be gone for long periods of time. When he returned home he would abuse Maria's mother. There were times when Maria's father would beat her brother, and if her mother tried to protect her son the father would take out his whip and punish her. The acts of abuse came to an end when Maria's father was arrested in 1937 by agents of the NKVD. Maria would not see him again.

Maria's life with her husband Yuri was a happy one. They worked hard and long hours to enjoy a good life. Beyond the responsibilities that came with their job titles as members of a collective farm, they were engaged in other activities to earn extra money. One such activity was gathering the sunflower seeds that fell to the ground at the time the sunflowers were harvested on the farm. Maria would collect several bags of seeds, take them home and winnow them, fry them and then bring them to a nearby city and sell them to the people in the streets. The kind of free enterprise practiced by Maria was permitted in Izmaelovka. With the money that Maria earned through the sale of sunflower seeds she was able to buy clothes and other items for Yuri and her children.

MARIA'S ACCOUNT

I was born in Izmaelovka and I have gotten old in the village, but my mind is healthy and my memory is clear and sharp. One of my earliest memories dates back to 1932 when I was just four years old. In that year my parents and

I left Izmaelovka to live in a commune. My father had been appointed an official of the commune. All the cattle in that commune were held in a common enclosure. The food in the commune was prepared in large cast-iron pots hanging from trivets over open fires. Everyone took their portions of food from these pots. Some ate at a common table, but others took their food and ate it in their homes. I remember eating boiled eggs and soup. When the commune became a collective farm it was called "Blukher," in honor of a military hero of the Civil War. After Blukher was denounced as an "enemy of the people," the collective farm was renamed "Stalin's Way" and today the village is called "The Sixth Branch."

Mother and I left the commune and returned to Izmaelovka without my father. My father was a handsome man; he was curly headed and could play the hand accordion. While we lived in the commune father was rarely home, and mother learned that he was seeing another woman. Later father would join us in Izmaelovka.

In Izmaelovka mother did a variety of jobs as a member of the collective farm. During haymaking time she worked on a mowing machine, and during harvest time she worked on a threshing machine. She earned "workdays" for the jobs that she completed. It was possible to earn more than one "workday" during a day's work. If a worker was required to mow 100 "sotkas" (2.5 acres of land) and that person mowed 120 "sotkas," the person would receive to her or his credit a 1.2 "workday." It was possible for a hard worker to earn in credit a 1.5 "workday" or 2 "workdays" during one day's work.

Workers like my mother were members of the farm's field brigades. During the sowing and harvest seasons these brigades stayed out on the fields day and night. The workers slept in small dwellings with wooden wheels that were rolled onto the fields. A dwelling could hold as many as six people and this was where the workers slept. In the mornings the workers would be awakened by the brigade leader, and after a quick breakfast they would begin their long workday. A brigade leader supervised the work of the brigade workers. The leader was appointed by the management board of the collective farm, and the management board was elected at a meeting attended by all the members of the collective farm.

Life became difficult when my father began to abuse mother and my brother. Father was a good felt boot maker, but he drank too much. Sometimes he would be gone for as long as a month. Upon his return home he would treat my mother and brother with contempt, mocking, taunting and insulting them. Father loved me very much; nevertheless, I hated how he treated my mother and brother. When my brother lost a penknife, my father sent him to Remnick's Forest to look for it. My brother got lost in the forest, and when he returned home many hours later without the penknife father threatened to kill him. Mother tried to protect her son, and father in turn gave her a terrible beating. On another occasion my father almost killed my brother with a harvesting machine. Again mother tried to protect my brother and this time father punished her by using a whip. "Are these the actions of a loving husband and father?"

In 1937 my father took a mysterious trip to Kizil. I did not know the purpose of the trip, and when father came home the people of the collective arranged a party to which the men brought bottles of vodka. At the party father asked me if I would sing with him. I said I would and so he placed me on one side of him and my brother on the other. Then I began singing a song titled "My Father was a Plower." The words of the song went as follows:

> My father was a plower by nature,
> And I worked together with him.
> He was arrested with the very first portion,
> And I stayed to be an orphan.

After I finished the song, I began to cry, and the people at the party began to weep as well. Father embraced me and asked me, "Why did this song come to mind?" I cried some more and then replied, "I do not know." Again he embraced me and looking into my eyes said, "Many of us will be arrested soon." At that time, I did not understand my father's comment. The questions of why and for what reason ran through my mind. Who could have guessed that he was foretelling the arrest of several village men including his own?

Prokophy Shirshov was one of the first men in the collective farm to be arrested by the NKVD. Our family knew him well because he was our neighbor. Prokophy was a watchman in the collective farm; he looked after the cows. He was often sick due to a stomach ailment, but in spite of his illness he would go to work. Late one evening two strangers came to his home and asked his wife about his whereabouts. She told them that he had left for his job. Prokophy worked during the night. The two men left and went after Prokophy. Mother and I were outside at the time, and we saw the neighbor's late evening visitors. The next morning mother went to see Prokophy's wife and asked her, "Anna, who were those men who asked about your husband?" Anna replied that after the visitors had left she and her son walked to Prokophy's work place, and there they were told that her husband had been arrested. Prokophy's family would never see him again. (Prokophy Shirshov was born in 1893 in Izmaelovka, was arrested on February 28, 1938 and was shot on April 22, 1938).

The arrest of Prokophy was followed by the arrests of others. Michael Shirshov, the brother of Prokophy, was arrested. Ivan Vasilievich was taken away.

Korsakov was arrested. I knew his family well. I used to wash their floors and take care of their children. Korsakov and his family were poor. Every person that was arrested, who I remember, was poor. It is my belief that the authorities arrested the poorest workers in the collective farm. They disappeared suddenly and at night; it was usually at night. The NKVD agents would drive up in a black police car, the so called "Black Raven," escort the victim from his home, put him in the car and drive away (see Glossary—Great Purge).

It was during the daytime that my father was arrested. It happened while I was away buying some things for mother at the village store. When I returned home, mother told me that father had been taken by the NKVD and that as they drove away he had tried to get out of the car. Mother said that she could hear him sing, "Oh. My dear fatherland, I shall never see you again...." Mother told my brother and me that she feared the NKVD would return and arrest us as well. We sat down beside her, and she embraced us and wept softly. She wondered out loud if we would be arrested separately or together. We sat together for a long time. We never saw father again, and it would be years later when I was informed about his death.

After the Communist Party fell from power in 1991, I began a search for my father's fate. I had learned that he had been sent to the Lukshinsky district of the Archanelsk region. I wrote the chief of the local police in the Lukshinsky district requesting that he send me documents concerning my father's death. The document that I received stated when and where my father died, but the cause of death was not recorded. The document was official confirmation of my father's death, and I wasted no time in going to a Russian Orthodox Church and asking the priest to arrange a funeral ceremony for my father and for my mother. I had not held a funeral ceremony for my mother because at the time of her death it was impossible to conduct a religious ceremony. The priest agreed to conduct a dual ceremony, and I invited my relatives to a commemorative feast. I also purchased a padded jacket for my son and a shirt for my son-in-law to remind them of their grandparents.

My uncle, Ivan Sergeevich, was apprehended several days after my father's arrest. He was my father's brother, and he lived on the collective farm called "Stalin's Way." We learned about his arrest when the police officer who made the arrest drove up to our house to tell mother that he was bringing Uncle Ivan to Kizil. The officer asked my mother for my father's documents. As mother handed the officer the documents she gave him some bread and tobacco to give to my father. I was told afterwards that the officer's name was Platonov and that he was a distant relative to mother. Before Platonov drove off, we heard my uncle within the police car make the statement that he was being arrested because of his brother.

Uncle Ivan was held by the NKVD for eighteen months and then was permitted to go home. Upon his release, his wife and daughter traveled to Kizil to get him. My uncle was too weak and crippled from the beatings he had received to walk home. When he arrived home, the entire family was overjoyed to see him. We had not expected to see him again. People wanted to know what had happened to him, but he refused to talk about the NKVD.

Years later Uncle Ivan would tell us at different times what the NKVD had done to him during their investigation of him. He described the terrible beatings that he suffered. Whenever they beat him into unconsciousness, they would pour cold water over him and continue the interrogation. He told us that once, after he had lost consciousness, they brought him into the cellar of the NKVD building. They thought they had killed him. When he recovered his consciousness, he saw several dead bodies in the cellar lying in puddles of blood. It was a miracle that he was still alive. Uncle Ivan was a stubborn man and would not confess to a lie. A denunciation used by the State against an "enemy of the people" required the signatures of at least forty-two witnesses. Uncle Ivan refused to sign a denunciation. For that they beat him terribly and turned him into a permanent cripple.

It was Alexander Stebelev, a native of Izmaelovka, who helped draft the denunciations used by the NKVD against the people from our village. Stebelev himself had been arrested and imprisoned in Kizil. In order to save himself, he cooperated with the NKVD and wrote down events that could be used to condemn a person who had been arrested. He would also forge signatures to get the necessary forty-two on a denunciation document.

There is evidence to believe that the chairman of our collective farm worked with the NKVD and arranged the arrests of my father and other men in the village. His name was Stepan Vasichkin, but people used his nickname "Vaga" whenever they addressed him. Cossacks gave each other nicknames while they were children, and they were expected to use those nicknames for life. Vaga had lots of informers within the collective farm, and they would report to him what they saw and heard. After a member of the village was arrested, the chairman of our collective farm, Vaga, would be summoned to Kizil to attend the interrogation that was conducted by the NKVD.

We did not know who the informers were, and we were careful to express our thoughts only to trusted friends. Many times the father of my friend, Pasha, warned us not to voice any complaints "because even the walls have ears." One day as Pasha and I opened a curtain in her parent's house, we saw a person standing outside near the window. He had been listening to our conversation. He covered his face and ran away. Two days later Pasha's father was arrested.

Vaga used bribes to protect himself and his position. Periodically, he would load down a wagon with food grown on the collective farm and bring the food to the Party officials in Kizil. The food was stolen from the farm's storehouses. Vaga also brought farm goods to his mistress who lived in Michaelovka. She told others about it after she and Vaga had a falling out. She claimed that Vaga would bring large chunks of meat wrapped in oilcloth to the authorities in Kizil. With these gifts he gained immunity from the repressive measures of the NKVD in the late 1930s. I am sure that Vaga was worried about his own welfare especially since his past actions could be used against him and lead to a denunciation. You see, back during the Civil War Vaga was a soldier in the White army commanded by General Dufor in 1917 and 1918. General Dufor's Cossack army fought against the Red Army. "How is it possible that a terrible person such as Vaga was chosen by the members of the collective to be their chairman?"

It was my schoolteacher who protected me from the consequences of being a daughter of an "enemy of the people." Her name was Nina Vasilievna and she had come from Magnitogorsk to teach in our village school. She knew that there were school children who, following my father's arrest, tried to ostracize me. I was in second grade at the time and Nina made it possible for me to become a member of the Young Pioneers organization (see Glossary—Young Pioneers). I was a good student and Nina made that known to the other students. However, I remember the times when classmates would kick me because my father was an "enemy of the people."

Going to school was more difficult in the winter than in the summer. In the winter I needed a coat, and I was able to acquire one in exchange for the fuel bricks that I made out of our cow's manure. The coat was old and ugly. One flap of the coat was longer than the other, and a large white patch had been sewn onto one of the sides. The patch was no problem because mother stripped off the jacket's outer covering, turned the jacket inside out and had me wear it that way. Mother used the jacket's outer covering to make me underwear. In the winter I also wore a shawl, which I had made out of wool that my uncle had given me. My brother and I had to share a pair of felt boots so only one of us could attend school on a school day.

In the summer I walked to school barefoot. I wore a printed calico dress, which was purposely bought too long so that I could use it several years and grow into it. My mother wore clothes that were similar to mine. We looked like beggars. Our clothes were appropriate since the origin of our surname, Nishchev, is *nishchii*, which means beggar. I do not forget that and make sure that when people come into my house they do not leave before having something to eat and drinking a cup of tea. It is I believe my duty to God.

I have believed in God since I can remember; however, I was not raised in a church. The church in the village was destroyed during collectivization. Izmaelovka had a beautiful church, and I remember watching the officials taking the icons out of the church and burning them. There were older people watching as well and they swore at the officials and condemned them for violating a holy place.

The priest of the church was arrested and taken away. His name was Uglichin. I would see him again several years later in Magnitogorsk. He was pointed out to me by mother who saw him from a distance digging a trench under the guard of armed soldiers and large dogs. She explained to me that our priest was a member of a prison brigade. He was wearing an old gray outfit, and his beard had been shaved off. It was this man who had baptized me. It is interesting that Maria was the name given to me at baptism, but my father who was a Communist renamed me Rosa in honor of Rosa Luxemburg. I prefer the name Maria (see Glossary—Luxemburg, Rosa).

Mother was not a believer and did not foster my faith in God. The only time I heard her mention God's name was on a wintry January evening. It was cold in the house, and she and I took our sickles and went outside to cut some dry weeds for fuel. The snow was high, and we had difficulty finding dry weeds. Finally, out of frustration, mother swore at God. Then she broke down and wept for a long time. Life had become too difficult for mother.

I was introduced briefly to a Bible as a child. The Bible was owned by an old woman and was written in the old Slavonic language. I saw it twice and read some of the stories. I remember how good that felt. When the old woman died in 1938 the Bible was placed in her coffin, and fifty years would pass before I would see another Bible. Throughout those years I would keep my faith in God a secret. I am convinced that if I had expressed my faith, I would have lost my job. Today, I own a Bible and read it faithfully and reread some of the stories that I read as a child in the old woman's Bible.

A family never experiences just one misfortune, and in 1939 mother, my brother and I would be able to attest to that. During the winter our cow disappeared. My brother and a relative rode into the nearby hills suspecting that the cow had wandered off. In the hills they met a hunter who told them that he had seen the remains of a cow, and standing near those remains was a well-fed wolf. At that time there were many wolves in the nearby hills. My brother and relative rode to the place where the hunter had seen the remains of a cow, and they found a black tail and some small pieces of skin. Mother cried bitterly about the loss of the cow because it was our only source of milk and butter.

In the spring one of the walls of our house fell to the ground. The wall, which was made of mud bricks, had been weakened by the melted snow and the spring rains. Nobody was home when it happened so no one was hurt; however, we could not continue living in our house. The wall would have to be repaired and that would take time and cost money.

Nikoljavich Kropotov was the chairman of the Village Council and he made available to mother a room, as a place to live, in a building used by the Village Council. He also gave mother a job working for the Village Council. He did not register her as a worker. I do not know why? Maybe it was dangerous for him to hire the wife of a man who had been denounced as an "enemy of the people."

I remember distinctly the day when the beginning of the war was announced. It was June 22, 1941. The announcement came over the radio in the Village Council office, and the women who were in the office began to cry. Shortly thereafter, I was ordered by the chairman of the Village Council to stay by the telephone in the Village Council office. He told me that a call might come in at any time with orders for certain men in the village to report for military duty in Kizil. If that should happen, it was my responsibility to find those men and give them their orders. The orders for military service did come through, and the secretary of the Village Council handed me the draft notices to give to the men who were to report to Kizil for military duty. On June 22, I delivered six draft notices.

In the days that followed, I would deliver many more draft notices. Most of the men who were drafted were working along the bank of the river with their wives making fuel bricks out of manure. When a draft notice arrived, I would run to the bank of the river to hand it to the rightful person. I was the bearer of bad news, and the people at the river bank hated to see me coming. They would stop their work and just watch me. Most of the men receiving a draft notice accepted it quietly, but their wives would cry bitterly. The men would leave the river bank immediately, walk home to get their necessary items and go to the village square where someone was waiting to transport them to Kizil. Within a short period of time, Izmaelovka had lost most of its men. Almost all of them went to war.

The old men, the women and the young boys and girls on the collective farm were required to fill the vacancies left by the men who were drafted into the military. Many of the young girls were sent to Obruchevka to study agricultural machines. Within a month they became tractor drivers and combine operators. I did not go to Obruchevka because I was too young. I continued working in the Village Council office.

In the spring of 1942, I joined a field brigade and was assigned to plow the agricultural fields with bulls. Sometimes I was told to plow virgin lands. A workday would begin an hour before sunrise, which was when the herdswoman arrived on the field with the bulls. She did not have a wrist watch; virtually no one in the village owned a wrist watch, yet she would arrive faithfully an hour before sunrise. She told us that she could tell the time by looking at the stars. After tethering the bulls, the herdswoman awakened us. We as members of the brigade slept together on wide planks covered by straw within a sheltered camp in the field. After being awakened we prepared the bulls for our morning work. Putting the heavy yoke on the bulls was difficult, and I was small in size. The plow was also heavy but the bulls were obedient. I would say to them: "Furrow! Follow the furrow!" They would then pull the plow, and I would follow them walking barefoot on the turned cold soil with a whip hanging on my arm. I never used the whip because I never found it necessary to use it.

The fields that I plowed were usually about two kilometers (1.2 miles) long. By the time I finished plowing the first furrow, daylight had arrived. When I returned to camp, having made my second furrow, a banner would be hanging from the field kitchen used by the brigade. It meant that breakfast was ready, and breakfast was followed by several more hours of plowing. At noon we were given another meal and a little time to rest, and the bulls were taken to the river by the herdswoman so that they could eat and drink. After the bulls were returned to the field, the work continued until our dinner break, which started around 6:00 P.M. I know that it began at 6:00 P.M. because I was able to determine the time by measuring the shadow that my body cast as I stood with my back to the sun. If the shadow was six feet long it was 6 o'clock, and it was time to go to dinner. After dinner we would plow until sunset.

On Saturday mornings we were permitted to go home to spend time with our families. I knew that mother would be hungry so I would not eat my Saturday breakfast that was served in the field kitchen. I would take that food home to give to mother. Saturday was a good day. It was a day to relax, to laugh, to bathe and to wash clothes. The next morning, before sunrise, mother would awaken me; we would say goodbye, and I would begin my walk to the field to start another week of work.

Because the meals that we were fed in the fields did not fully sustain us, we made "kurmatch" and ate that as well. "Kurmatch" was wheat seeds that had been fried in a bucket over an open fire of dried manure. The seeds belonged to the collective farm, and eating them was forbidden. Our brigade leader was an old man, a veteran of the Civil War. He was held responsible for the wheat seeds, but he recognized our hunger and sympathized with us. He told us that if we should take some seeds to make "kurmatch" he did not want to know about it, and he warned us to be on the constant lookout for Party representatives from Kizil. If they caught us making "kurmatch" we might be arrested and imprisoned. A person who was found guilty of stealing one kilogram of seeds might be imprisoned for a year.

In our brigade it was Anna Ivanovna Alemanova who prepared the "kur-match" for the entire brigade. We worked on the open steppe so we could see an approaching car a long distance away. Whenever that happened we would warn Anna, and she would quickly hide the stolen seeds. At the end of the workday, Anna would take home the "kurmatch" that was left over. Anna had three hungry children at home, and they too were sustained on the stolen seeds. In order to avoid getting caught, Anna hid the seeds in the sleeves of her padded jacket before going home.

Our brigade leader would always have wheat bread when it was time to eat. "Where did his wife get the wheat to make the bread?" The brigade leader must have acquired the wheat from the collective farm storage building. We did not know how he was able to do this, but it was done because no one in the village at that time was given wheat to eat. Later, when the collective farm began storing millet in the storage buildings, the brigade leader came to work with bread made from millet.

During harvest time several of us young girls were assigned the job of winnowing wheat. We did this for many hours every day, and I became good at it. Just imagine how many times each of us had to bend down everyday to get a spade full of wheat and throw that wheat high into the air.

In the wintertime, I along with others worked as milkmaids in the stockyard. Each of us was assigned twelve cows. It was our responsibility to prepare silage and feed the cows. We were also required to milk them and this was done by hand. In the winter we also sheared the sheep owned by the collective farm.

All the people in Izmaelovka worked for victory. While the fathers, brothers and sons of the village were fighting, we planted and harvested the wheat that was used to feed them. We also put together parcels, and these too were sent to the soldiers. Sometimes as many as eight of us girls would gather in a house in the winter evenings and knit socks, mittens, tobacco pouches and other items for the soldiers. The yarn that we used was made from hemp that we had harvested and processed. The authorities did not tell us to make the parcels; we did this at our own initiative. Getting together and making parcels was fun. We would talk, share our dreams and sing songs. The adult women in the village also got together to make parcels.

Hemp was used extensively during the war years. We collected the hemp seeds, winnowed them, ground them into flour and used the flour to make scones. The hemp stalks were harvested as well and placed in the river. They were then heated and dried in the village bathhouse. After that the dried stalks were pounded, smashed and combed. The best fibers were spun into yarn, and the other fibers were waxed and used as wicks in our oil lamps.

Mother and I lighted our oil lamps with the smoldering ashes taken from the fire within the house stove. If the fire went out, I would have to go to our neighbor's house and acquire from her some smoldering ashes. We had no matches during the war years. Later on, we would make our own matches by dipping small sticks of dry wood into liquid sulphur.

It was a time of rejoicing whenever one of the men from the village came home on leave of absence for several days. These times of joy were rare because more often the village would receive a "vikluchka," which was an official notification of a soldier's death. Then there was much weeping in the village.

In 1944 the chairman of the Village Council received orders from Kizil to send several young people in the village to Magnitogorsk to become industrial workers. Alexandre, Nikolai, Olga and I were sent. When we arrived in Magnitogorsk, we were told that we were not needed there and that we should go on to the city of Chelyabinsk (see Glossary-Chelyabinsk). When we reached Chelyabinsk, we decided together to disobey our orders and take the train back to Magnitogorsk and then find our way back to Izmaelovka. We were hungry, but we had no money to buy food. We begged for money at the Chelyabinsk railway station but with little success. The people we approached had almost nothing themselves. In Gusevka, which was on the way to Magnitogorsk, we were given two potatoes by someone who felt sorry for us, and the four of us shared the potatoes.

Upon our arrival in Magnitogorsk, a woman on the train advised us to avoid the city railway station and leave the city as quickly as possible. She explained that there were military patrols at the railway station that were looking for military deserters. At this time, draftees from Middle Asia were being transported by train to the military front in eastern Europe, and many of these men would try to leave the trains and desert at the railway stations. Those who succeeded gathered in gangs and lived as outlaws, robbing, raping and killing.

The woman on the train warned us to watch out for the deserters and for the military patrols. She showed us how to leave Magnitogorsk by following the railroad tracks and walking between the trains. We took her warning and advice seriously and after we got off the train we began making our way back to Izmaelovka. It was November and it was freezing cold, and when we finally arrived in Izmaelovka I was sick. For a long time I tried to get over the illness by eating goose fat.

When Olga returned to Izmaelovka, her stepfather told her that she would have to return to Magnitogorsk. He placed her in a cart, brought her to Magnitogorsk and left her there. She was a young girl alone in a large industrial city. She was afraid. She told me later that a man picked her up and provided her with a place to live. He waited until she was sixteen years old and then lived and slept with her. She gave birth to a girl. Since then the man died, but Olga still lives in Magnitogorsk in a nice apartment, and she has plenty of money.

Victory Day was May 9, 1945. I remember hearing a loud voice on the radio at the Village Council building announcing that fascist Germany had surrendered, and the war was over. People laughed, embraced and wept. It was a wonderful day. However, the "vikluchkas" continued coming, and only a few men returned home. There were many widows in the village, and only a few remarried. My brother came home but left the village shortly thereafter and moved to Novopototsk, a village in the Orenburg region.

After the war the chairmen of the Village Council received orders from Kizil to send several young village people to an industrial workers' school. The chairman wanted to send me, but I did not want to go. My trip to Magnitogorsk and Chelyabinsk back in 1944 had cured me of wanting to live in a city. I told the chairman that I would go if my friend Lena agreed to go with me. The chairman promised that he would ask Lena to go also and that gave me some time to plan my escape. I left the village secretly early the next morning with a relative who was going to Amour. From Amour I traveled to Novopototsk and joined my brother.

I lived in Novopototsk for two years, and I still remember that village with fondness. It was a quiet community. Nobody in Novopototsk was arrested by the NKVD or by the police. No one in this village was sent to the city against her or his will. There was a shortage of workers in the village, and because of my previous working experience I was given the job of milkmaid.

In early 1947 my brother suggested that we go to Izmaelovka to persuade our mother to live with us in Novopototsk. "It is not good for her to live alone," he said. I told him that I was afraid to return to Izmaelovka because earlier I had deceived the chairman of the Village Council, and since then the village considered me a refugee. My brother told me not to worry and so I accompanied him to our former village; we brought mother back with us to Novopototsk. Mother was ill and on July 19, 1947, she died. We buried her in Novopototsk.

In the autumn I received a letter from my aunt in Izmaelovka stating that she was ill and requesting that I come and take care of her. I loved my aunt and was afraid that she was suffering from the same illness from which mother had died. I made plans to leave for Izmaelovka as soon as I was permitted. Occasionally, someone in Novopototsk would travel by cart to Izmaelovka, and I succeeded in getting there in this way. On the way to Izmaelovka we stopped in Iliaska where I overheard some working girls say, "Look, the bride has arrived." I asked them if they were referring to me and who was to be the bridegroom. They replied that Iniakin was to be the bride-groom, and I was to be his wife. I was shocked and tried to quiet the beating of my heart. I wondered why I had not been told about this and asked the girls how my aunt was feeling. "She's fine," they answered. The answer was puzzling. When I arrived at my aunt's house I asked her why she had urged me to come. She replied that it had been a trick to get me to come to Izmaelovka to meet Yuri Iniakin, my future husband.

My courtship with Yuri lasted four days. It began in the evening of the day of my arrival in Izmaelovka. One of my friends came to my aunt's house and asked me to take a walk with her. We walked to the village school, which was a meeting place for the young people, and along the way we met another one of my friends. She told me that she knew about the scheme to get me to Iz-maelovka to become Yuri's bride. It is typical of life in a village, everyone knows everything about everybody. As we walked near the school building a third friend ran up and said, "Look! Your bridegroom, Yuri, is standing over there." I blushed, turned away and walked back to my aunt's house. My aunt was already sleeping when I returned, and as I was preparing to go to bed I heard a knock on the door. I re-buttoned my blouse, opened the door and saw Yuri standing at the doorway. He came in, and we sat till morning talking to each other and laughing. When my aunt awakened she made us breakfast, and then Yuri went to work.

Yuri came to visit me again on the second and third evenings. He told me that it was his mother who had urged him to ask me to be his wife. She had said that it was foolish to go looking for a bride when Masha (Maria) is avail-able. You cannot find, she had said, a better wife. Masha, she pointed out, has no mother and I have no daughter; it will be good for us to live together. I be-lieve that Yuri's mother must have liked me because of the times when I vis-ited her as a young girl. She must have remembered that I had often combed her hair and examined it carefully for lice. I never found any lice because she kept her hair clean. In order to further justify our marriage, Yuri reminded me that he had known me as an infant. It was true. He and my brother had been friends, and there had been times when he would come to our house and take care of me. Finally, he said that he loved me. He asked me to marry him on the second evening.

On the fourth evening Yuri's mother came to my aunt's house to propose of-ficially a marriage between Yuri and me. We agreed to the marriage and decided that October 16 was to be the wedding day. Yuri promised to find me a wedding dress, and he found a nice one. It was important to me that the dress look nice, and Yuri must have realized that because after we were married he always tried to buy me a nice dress whenever I needed one. I never "painted" my hair be-cause it was black, and I never "painted" my face, but I did wear lipstick.

I knew that my brother would not be pleased that I had agreed to marry Yuri. I had made an important decision without his advice. When I returned to Novopototsk and told my brother about my plans to marry Yuri, he replied, "What does this mean? You leave home for a couple of days, and in the meantime you find a bridegroom. I do not want to hear a word about it. If you want to marry, we will find a bridegroom here in Novopototsk." My brother's response was upsetting; it destroyed the happiness that I had carried with me from Izmaelovka. My brother then asked who it was that had proposed to me. He was surprised to find out that it was Yuri. He was surprised because he did not know that Yuri had returned from the war.

The situation became more complicated because of what my sister-in-law did. She went to her mother and told her that I was planning to marry Yuri. Within a short period of time, all the people of Novopototsk knew about Yuri and me.

One evening there appeared at my brother's house a young man, the "svat," and a young woman, the "svakha," representing a young man in Novopototsk who wanted to marry me (see Glossary—svat and svakha). They talked with my brother, and my brother promised them my hand in marriage. He did this without conferring with me. I asked my brother why he had done this, and his response was that according to tradition a bridegroom must send a "svat" and "svakha" to ask the oldest man in the future bride's family for the young woman's hand in marriage. Yuri had not done that; thus my brother did not consider him a genuine bridegroom. My brother informed me that my wedding to the young man in Novopototsk was scheduled for the fourteenth of October.

On the following day, I received a note from Yuri. The note was handed to me by a relative of Yuri. The note said that he would come to get me in a cart that would be drawn by bulls. Yuri did not know about my predicament. He did not know that I had been given by my brother to a young man in Novopototsk. I was also offended by Yuri's note. I knew that Yuri did not have a lot of money, but it was customary for a wedding cart to be pulled by a pair of beautifully dressed horses. In my responding note to Yuri, I asked why he was coming for me with bulls. "It is a disgrace," I wrote, "I will not go with bulls. Do you consider me a girl or a woman?"

Yuri received my note and came immediately to Novopototsk to talk with me. I told Yuri about my predicament. He told me not to worry and promised to come and get me on our wedding day with a cart pulled by dressed horses. After Yuri returned to Izmaelovka, I informed the young man who had been promised my hand in marriage by my brother that I would not marry him. I told him I was leaving Novopototsk and returning to my native village of Izmaelovka.

Our wedding was wonderful. Yuri arrived in Novopotosk on the evening of October 15 with a wedding cart pulled by horses that were dressed with bells. The "druzka" followed him (see Glossary—druzka). Later that night we broke with tradition by having a wedding feast at my brother's house. It was customary to arrange the first wedding feast in the house of the bridegroom. In the morning the relatives of my sister-in-law arranged another pair of dressed horses for me and my belongings, and we went to Izmaelovka where we were welcomed by Yuri's relatives and my girl friends. Back then I had a strong voice and could sing beautifully so I sang, "Where are you, my darling?" All of my friends wept.

The second wedding feast was attended by my relatives. Yuri and I sat at the head of the main table. My aunt and my mother-in-law sat on each side of us, and next to them sat my brother and his wife and then our closest relatives. The food that was served at the feast had been grown or raised on the collective farm. We had bread, potatoes, cabbage, beetroot soup, noodles, tomatoes, cucumbers and other foods. During the meal the guests raised their drinks to love, happiness, health and many years of marriage. Yuri kissed me, which signified to the guests that I was a virgin and still sweet. At the close of the second day of feasting, the guests retired and Yuri and I spent our first night together as husband and wife in my mother-in-law's house. Again we broke with tradition because it was customary for newly weds to spend their first night together in a house that would not be their future place of residence.

Early the next morning Yuri's "druzka" and my "svashka" awakened us and checked the bed sheets for bloodstains. It was a terrible disgrace if a bride was not a virgin. The "druzka" and "svashka" were to bring the sheets to the bride's mother so that she could examine them as well. My mother was dead, so the sheets were brought to my aunt. After that the "svashka" was to keep the sheets until the evening. Nobody was permitted to touch them.

Our third day of feasting began with a meal of pancakes prepared by my aunt. It was customary to have a breakfast of pancakes on the second day of feasting, but again we broke with tradition. During the meal of pancakes the bridegroom was supposed to break a plate, which signified that his bride had been an obedient wife. The guests were supposed to respond by shouting "bitter, bitter, bitter," which signified that the bride was no longer a virgin. After the meal the "svashka" was supposed to present to the guests the bed sheets that she had examined earlier that morning. As she approached the guests in the room, she cried out, "The passage is too narrow to bring the bedding in." The guests then gave her a glass of vodka and stepped aside to permit her to enter. The guests then drank, sang songs, danced and conducted what might be called a masquerade. The young women and girls dressed up as men, and the men put on women's clothes. They hung a sled on the gate and splashed each other with pails of water. There were many such activities especially after the guests had consumed a lot of home-brew.

Our home-brew had been prepared by my brother. He had made it out of wheat and sugar. He had placed three kilograms of wheat in a thirty-six liter milk churn and then added two large pails of warm water and one kilogram of sugar. Then he allowed it to ferment and would periodically add some more sugar. When the fermentation process ended, the liquid was removed, distilled and ready to be enjoyed. Sometimes we would drink the liquid without distilling it. I must admit that I was no saint, and I knew, everybody knew, that making home-brew was illegal. Those who were caught making home-brew were imprisoned. Our local policeman sent to prison his own mother-in-law for making home-brew.

After the wedding I stayed home for a month and became pregnant with my daughter, Katia. I gave birth to Katia in the maternity building in Izmaelovka and remained there a week. I was permitted to stay longer to nurse my baby, but we needed my income so I went back to work milking cows at the collective farm stockyard. My mother-in-law took care of my baby daughter, and at different times throughout the day I would run home to breast feed her. Often I would get home too late, and Katia would not like my milk. It was probably spoiled because after a while I experienced problems with my breasts.

Yuri and I worked hard in the hope of gaining a better life for our family. Of course we received wheat for the days that we worked, but we also tried to earn money. Yuri was such a quick learner; he needed to be shown just once how to do something, and after that he could do it. We also collected sunflowers. The collective farm had large fields of sunflowers, and there were usually many seeds in the fields following the harvest. I would take three or four empty sacks with me and go out to the fields to pick up the seeds. It was not difficult to fill four sacks. When I brought the seeds home, I winnowed the seeds, my mother-in-law fried them and then we sold them. Once we brought eight sacks of sunflowers to Sibai and sold them. With this money we bought clothes and other necessities.

My mother-in-law lived with us, and she and I would often talk about events that had happened in our area before I was born. She was a Communist and happy with the Soviet regime. Her husband was a Cossack who had served in the tsar's army. She told me that toward the beginning of 1917 he came home and told his relatives that important changes would take place in Russia. He said that his commanding officer had told him that the tsar would be removed from the throne, and a republic would be created in Russia. His relatives were surprised; they had not heard about such matters. After my father-in-law left the village to return to his military duties, the February Revolution took place and Tsar Nicholas II abdicated.

During the Civil War both White troops and Red soldiers passed through Izmaelovka. The Reds might come into the village in the morning and leave, and in the afternoon White soldiers would enter the village. My mother-in-law told me that neither the Whites nor the Reds harmed the people in Izmaelovka. If the Whites remained in the village overnight they would stay in the houses of women whose husbands served in a White army. The Reds stayed in the houses of men who were fighting in the Red Army. My mother-in-law said that she provided overnight lodging to soldiers who fought in the Red Army.

My mother-in-law remembered well the Great Hunger of 1921. Collectivization had not yet begun and my father-in-law was chairman of Izmaelovka's administrative board. During the Great Hunger he would go to the cemetery every morning to rebury the remains of people who had recently died and had been buried. During the night the people of the village would go to the cemetery and dig up these dead bodies and eat them. The people were so hungry that they resorted to cannibalism.

It was from my mother-in-law that I learned about Joseph Stalin's death. She announced his death when I came home for dinner. She said, "Stalin died," and then began to cry. I cried too. At that time, in 1953, we did not know about Stalin's cruelty. We did not know that it was Stalin who had given the orders that led to the arrests of many people including my father (see Glossary—Great Purge).

In 1954, my son, Sasha, was born. At that time, the maternity building in Izmaelovka was closed so I gave birth to Sasha in my home with the assistance of a midwife. Sasha's birth was easier than my first because in 1954 a mother was given a two-month maternity leave, one month before giving birth and one month after birth.

Yuri decided to build a new house after the birth of our son, Sasha. He constructed it in his spare time and did it alone because we could not afford to hire someone to help him. We purchased wood and bought sheets of metal, which were used to make the roof. After the frame of the house was finished, I plastered the walls with a mixture of yellow clay, sand and horse manure. It was finished in 1957. It had taken us three years to complete the house. We furnished it with a newly purchased closet, sofa and cupboard and some chairs.

Life in the village improved substantially in the 1950s. The improvements began with the changes made by Georgi Malenkov (see Glossary—Khrushchev, Nikita). It was he who abolished many of the taxes, which were so burdensome. For example, every family was required to give to the State annually 300 liters of milk, 100 eggs, 32 kilograms of meat and some wool. These requirements were abolished. Yuri told me that Malenkov had declared, "The Russian people must stop living in humiliation."

After Nikita Khrushchev replaced Melankov a number of programs were initiated that did more harm than good. Khrushchev's most harmful program was the cultivation of virgin lands on the steppes of Siberia. Before the program was put into effect, the steppes were covered with many grasses, flowers and strawberries. Then the steppes were plowed, seeds were planted and for three years the Soviet Union enjoyed excellent harvests of wheat. However, the environment had been changed. Erosion marred the land, and the soil lost its fertility. The consequences of Khrushchev's program had been foreseen by my mother-in-law when the program was first begun. "Why are they plowing these virgin lands?" she would ask. She was much more knowledgeable than me about such matters. I believed initially that Khrushchev's program would be beneficial. The more land that is plowed, I reasoned, the more wheat will be harvested. I was so foolish (see Glossary- Khrushchev's virgin lands program).

At the close of the 1950s I was forced to give up my job as a milkmaid. The work of a milkmaid was hard. I was required to milk twenty-seven cows three times a day by hand. In addition to that, I had to feed the calves and work in the silo. It was too much. Milking by hand caused my fingers to become twisted. I went to see the doctor about my hands, and he told me that I was suffering from brucellosis. He said I could not continue working as a milkmaid. The diagnosis was difficult for me to accept because I loved my cows. Thus, for a while, after I had stopped milking I would weep whenever I saw the village milkmaids walk to the stockyard. My new job was working as a cook in the village canteen.

Yuri and I were proud to be Russians, and this pride was bolstered through various achievements. We were proud when we learned that Yuri Gagarin had been launched into space successfully. It was Yuri who told me about this amazing achievement when I came home from work on April 12, 1961. That evening we listened to Gagarin speak on the radio (see Glossary-Gagarin, Yuri).

We were also proud of the Soviet Union's military achievements. We were convinced that the Soviet army was the strongest military force in the world; it gave us such a sense of security. We hated war and believed that a strong Soviet army would guarantee peace. We never believed that the Soviet army would be used in an aggressive way.

One of the saddest days of my life was the day that Yuri died. His death was the result of a job related accident. Yuri worked as a blacksmith in the village machine-repair shop. The men in the shop had made a large metal structure that had to be lifted to a vertical position. On the day that they were to do this the crane operator was drunk. The chief of the state farm insisted that the job be done anyway and without the crane. The weight of the structure was about 3.5 tons. As the men raised the structure Yuri noticed that the bottom of the structure was slipping from its base, and he went to warn the men about it. At that moment the structure fell on its side and on top of Yuri and another worker. Yuri's body was folded together like a closed penknife. When the workers raised the metal structure off of Yuri he was in such pain that he spun like a top and uttered terrible language. I was home and washing clothes when the son of the village policeman came running and yelled "Aunt Masha, come quickly, Uncle Yuri is in the medical building." (The words uncle and aunt were used by the children in the village to address adults. It was a sign of respect). I ran to the medical building and was told about the accident. Yuri did not want to stay there so I brought him to the hospital in Magnitogorsk. The doctor told me that Yuri's pancreas had been damaged, and if Yuri was to live the pancreas would have to be replaced with one that was man-made. I desperately wanted the doctor to do this and so I brought the doctor some

Maria Grigorievna is wearing the traditional padded jacket and is standing next to her house in Izmaelovka.

geese as a bribe. He would not take the geese, but he agreed to perform the operation anyway and said that if it proved to be a success he would take the geese as a gift of thanks. The damaged pancreas was replaced, and Yuri lived another year and a day. I then became a widow. The year was 1974.

After Yuri's death, I was given a job as cook in the village school cafeteria. I worked at this job for several years before I, like Yuri, suffered an accident. The accident took place on August 30, 1981. On that day the chairman of the Village Council told me and four other workers in the school cafeteria to go to a potato field and dig up potatoes that were to be served in the cafeteria. We were to go in a small low van that was driven by a young fellow who I did not know. The four of us sat in the dark in the enclosed rear area of the van and sang songs as we were driven to the potato field. Suddenly, we felt the van slide down the slippery slope along the road, and then we hit a bump that threw me into the roof of the van. I lost consciousness while my fellow workers were knocking on the rear wall of the van's cabin to get the driver to stop. When I recovered my consciousness, the driver offered to take me to the village medical building. I told him that I would try to help dig up potatoes and so we rode on. When we reached the potato field I lost consciousness again. It was the leader of the tractor brigade that took me by tractor back to the village and to the medical building. By that time my feet had lost all feeling.

I spent the next three years in the medical building. Toward the end of the first year I was able to move my toes. Then little by little I succeeded in sitting, standing and walking. The workers at the medical building treated me with great care, and after the third year I was able to return home and continue working. I was unable to work at a job that required heavy lifting so I became the nurse at the village school. I worked at that job until I was permitted to retire with a pension.

Chapter Five

"Unhappy Wife"

Nina Kozhevnikova

Life for Nina as a young girl and as a teenager was not easy. Her father died when she was just five years old and she and her mother were forced to live simply, gathering or making that which they needed. In the summer season Nina would gather from the steppes of the Ural region the plants from which she would make brooms to sweep the floors. The soap that she used to wash her clothes was made from the bones of animals that had been slaughtered in the village. The dresses and the skirts and blouses that Nina wore were made by her mother from fabrics purchased in the nearest city. Periodically the mud brick building that was home for Nina and her mother needed to be repaired, and it was Nina who made the repairs using the clay that she gathered from the clay pits near Izmaelovka. Because cloth was expensive, Nina and her mother did not cover the windows of their house with curtains but with old newspapers that they had cut in a decorative manner.

Nina began working after she graduated from the fourth grade. Her first job was taking care of the village calves. She would awaken before sunrise, walk to the cow barn and feed the calves. She would remain with the animals all day except to go home to eat her afternoon meal. Nina next worked as a caretaker of the village pigs arriving at the pig pens each morning to clean the pigs and feed them. When Nina became a milkmaid she was assigned to milk more than twenty cows twice each day. It was hard work, but Nina was not afraid of hard work. There were many times when she would volunteer to do additional work for the collective farm. As a reward for her volunteerism, Nina was given gifts of appreciation such as dresses and stockings. One year Nina was awarded by the farm administrators the medal "For Valiant Labor."

NINA'S ACCOUNT

My parents were poor. Maria Nesterova was my mother's name and she was born in the 1910s. Alexander Pleshkov was my father's name and he was born in 1916. I have only a few personal recollections of him. He was drafted into military service shortly after I was born, was wounded in battle and was returned home before the war ended. He died in 1944. I was five years old at the time.

Most of what I know about my father was told to me by my mother. She said that my grandfather had a mistress at the time that my father's mother gave birth to him. My grandfather wanted to get rid of my grandmother so he murdered her shortly after my father was born. He did this by adding arsenic to a glass of water that she had requested. She was thirsty for she had just given birth. She died and was buried, and no cause of death was established because there was no doctor in the area to examine the body.

My father was raised by my grandfather and his mistress. Mother told me that my father's mistress did not love him. There were times when she would not permit him to sleep in the house so my father would sleep with the calves. Once he ran away from home. It was wintertime and bitter cold, and father collapsed. He would have died, but a Kazakh on horseback saw him lying in the snow. He picked him up, placed him on his horse and brought him back to the village and home. The Kazakh had saved his life.

When father was old enough to leave home he moved to Izmaelovka. Here he was made the caretaker of the Village Club. He was probably given that position because he was a good hand accordionist. The accordion was usually played when people would gather together to sing and dance at the Village Club. It was while working in Izmaelovka that my father met mother. Shortly after their wedding the war began, and father was sent to the front. He was injured and sent home and then was appointed the manager of a village named Novinka.

Men who were my father's superiors would periodically come to Novinka. Once a group of men dressed in military uniforms stayed at our house. When I asked who these people were, mother simply said that they were the men in charge. Just before their visit some village sows had given birth to piglets, and father gave to each of our guests a piglet. Several days later the guests arrived in the village again. Mother invited them to supper to eat a meal of salted mushrooms and boiled potatoes. Following the meal the men began to laugh. "Alexander," they asked, "what should we do with you? The reason we have returned to the village is to arrest you for stealing the state farm's piglets!" "Well," my father replied, "arrest me, if it is necessary." "How can we arrest you," they asked, "when you gave them to us, especially since you did not keep a piglet for yourself?" Apparently someone had reported to the authorities that my father had stolen several piglets from the state farm. Whoever had reported my father's theft did not know that the piglets had been given to the authorities to whom the theft was reported.

Life was hard during the last years of the war, and sometimes people would commit crimes out of desperation. Mother told me that father uncovered such a crime after he arrived at his office early one morning. He noticed a woman leaving the village carrying a child in her arms. He thought it was odd that she was out so early in the morning so he left his office and walked in the direction she had taken. When he arrived at the village stockyard he saw the woman again, but she did not have the child with her. She looked sad and her eyes were red from crying. Father asked her where her child was, but she did not answer; she just wept. Father continued to press her on the child's whereabouts until she told him what she had done. She said that she had placed a heavy stone on the body of the child to kill it so that it would not have to die from hunger. Father immediately got an assistant and then ordered the woman to show them the location of her child. The stone covering the child was heavy, but after much difficulty it was removed. The child, however, was already dead.

As the manager of Novinka my father always wore his military uniform. He wore the long overcoat and the artificial fur hat with a red star on the front of it. He slept in the overcoat when it was cold and slept on it when the weather was warm. He used the hat as a pillow.

I remember that the war's end brought both joy and sorrow. The joy was immediate and conspicuous on Victory Day. On that day the people in our village gathered in the streets. Music was played by someone who owned an accordion, and the people laughed, sang songs and danced. The day of great joy was followed by days of sorrow when the fates of the village soldiers became known. We were told, for example, that "Romanenko returned home without his legs." I did not know Romanenko or the many other soldiers who were scarred by the war, but I could imagine their painful circumstances.

Mother and I lived in a primitive village named Zdanovka in the years after the war. There was no electricity in the village. We did not even have matches with which to light our stove in the morning. I remember that there were winter mornings when I would leave our house and go looking for a nearby house that had smoke coming out of its chimney. When I spotted such a house, I would ask the family inside for fire. They would give me a smoldering stick, and mother and I would use that to light our stove.

Mother and I had a mud brick house. The entrance to the house was an enclosed porch. Along the left end of the porch was a bin in which we stored our wheat. On the right end there was another bin that held our milled flour.

Both of the bins were left uncovered so that their contents would not turn moldy. On the far right side was the door to the only room in the house. It was used as a kitchen, living room and bedroom. Against the far left wall of the room was a chest for clothes, a bench and a table. Above the table hanging from the wall near the corner was an icon of the Virgin Mary. At the far right corner we had a mirror that had been given to us by my uncle. Along the right wall of the room there were two stoves that shared a single smoke duct. We had a Holland stove and a Russian stove.

The Russian stove was used to heat the house and for baking bread. Mother would begin baking bread some two hours before sunrise. She would light the stove and place the leavened dough, which she had prepared the evening before, into the oven of the stove. When I was awakened for breakfast, two hours later, the fresh hot bread was ready to be eaten. It was delicious. Along with the bread we would sometimes drink "kvass."

"Kvass" was a popular drink in the village. It was made with pieces of old bread, some yeast and warm water. These ingredients were mixed in a large milk churn and left to ferment for several days. Thereafter, it was placed in the cellar to cool, and after it was the right temperature it was poured in a glass. "Kvass" was a refreshing drink especially on a hot day.

Our Russian stove was also used to make soup. Mother would begin making the soup right after breakfast. If it was a vegetable soup such as beet root (borsch) or cabbage soup she would place the vegetable along with some meat in a large cast-iron kettle filled with water and hang the kettle over the fire in the stove for several hours. Our midday meal was usually soup.

Our suppers varied according to the season. In the fall, winter and spring months we would eat boiled potatoes or noodles with milk. We also ate scones or pies that mother prepared and baked in the morning when she made bread. The pies usually contained potatoes with carrots and onions. In the summer mother would bake strawberry and cherry pies. The fruits were wild and had been picked in the nearby forest. Pies with meat or fish were baked only on holidays. With each of our meals we would have a hot drink made with sage. We did not begin drinking tea until the latter 1960s, which was when the village store began selling tea.

During the summer we would gather from the steppes plants that were made into brooms. One variety of plant was green in color, and the brooms that were made with this plant were used to sweep the dirt around the house. Another plant which was white in color was used to make brooms with which we would sweep the floors inside the house. Many plants were gathered because each broom included some forty plants that were bound together with strong thread. A broom, if used often, would not last long so we made several of each type. In the 1970s brooms that were made in State owned enterprises began to appear in the village store. Thereafter, the people bought these brooms and stopped making their own.

We had no curtains for our two windows because we could not afford to buy the cloth to make the curtains. We hated the idea that somebody could observe us and our actions through the windows especially in the evening when the living room was illuminated. One day mother brought home some old newspapers that had been given to her by the people who worked at the collective farm administrative office. We cut the newspapers in a decorative way and covered the windows with our creations. We thought our window coverings were beautiful. We failed, however, to realize the danger in doing this. If one of the newspapers had included a portrait of Joseph Stalin and if his portrait had been cut by our scissors we would have suffered serious consequences.

Because our home was made of mud and mud bricks it had to be repaired every year. It was my responsibility to repair it. At the nearby village of Izmaelovka there were two large pits of white clay, and I would take from one pit the clay that I needed to repair the house walls and from the other pit the clay that I needed to repair the roof. It was wonderful clay, and I would mix into it straw which would prevent the clay, after it had hardened, from cracking. The fresh clay that was used to repair the roof was applied to the thick layer of old hardened clay that covered the willow rods that made up the base layer of the roof. The willow rods were three meters in length and had been laid crosswise from the top of the house walls to a higher log that extended across the middle of the house.

We did not have a bathhouse so a neighbor family invited us to use theirs every Saturday. The bathhouse, like most of the bathhouses in the village, was a small building located behind and away from the owner's residence. The building consisted of two rooms. The entrance was the anteroom and was furnished with a small bench. It was in this room where the bather would undress and hang her clothes over the wooden pegs on the wall. It was in this room where the bather, several hours before, had started a fire in the stove, which was designed to heat the sauna room of the bathhouse. The bather fed the stove with wood by opening the cast iron door that covered the mouth of the stove, which protruded through the wooden wall that separated the anteroom from the sauna room. The stove's belly, made out of stones, was in the sauna room, and when this room was heated to the desired temperature the bather would enter the room and pour some cold water from a cast iron kettle onto the hot stones of the stove. The room would fill quickly with steam and as it did the bather would give herself a massage by beating her body with a birch besom. There was a tub and a basin in the sauna as well, and in the winter I would wash my clothes in the tub. I owned just one dress so I would wash it quickly, wait for it to dry and then put it back on before leaving.

We washed our clothes with soap that was made in the village. In the spring the people of the village would take the bones of animals that had been butchered the previous spring and place the bones in brine. The bones would then be boiled for an entire day. After that the mixture would be cooled, and then the villagers, using long knives, would cut the cooled mixture into blocks. The blocks would then be dried and would be used to wash clothes. If there was no homemade soap, we used white clay to wash the clothes. We had no special washing board so we washed the clothes by hand. Washboards and manufactured soap would appear in the village store later. At that time, the villagers were also introduced to toilet soap. If we could not afford toilet soap, we would wash ourselves with homemade soap or milk that had the butter content extracted from it.

There was little variety in fashion when it came to clothes. The young girls and women in the village wore homemade dresses or skirts with blouses. Women did not wear trousers; they were considered men's clothes. In the summer the women would walk barefoot. Some girls wore sport shoes made of white textile with white rubber soles. When these shoes became dirty they would be cleaned with tooth powder and a toothbrush. In the winter the women would wear felt boots or rubber boots. I had rubber boots that I would dry in the rectangular hollows that had been made for this purpose in our Russian stove. In the house I would walk barefoot, and if mother asked me to go to a neighbor's house on a quick errand I would go in bare feet. The snow felt soft and wonderful as I walked through it.

Black velvet jackets were very popular with the women of the village. In the 1950s the Soviet industry produced hundreds of thousands of these jackets. However, it was difficult to get one, and those who did felt they had something very fashionable. The price of one of these jackets was seventy rubles, which was more than a month's salary for a state farm worker.

There were village women who were concerned about their appearance, and they tried to look more attractive. They did not use cosmetics such as eye shadow or colored powders to apply to their cheeks because they were not available, but they did color their lips using a red pencil. They also cut their hair in an attractive style, and later in the 1960s the village women would travel to Magnitogorsk to have a professional hairdresser put a permanent wave in their hair. Even I, in spite of the fact that I was married and had children, did this in order to look more attractive.

The school that I attended in Zdanovka included grades one through four. Because there was only one classroom in the school building, the first and second grade students were taught as one class in the morning, and the students in grades three and four were taught in the afternoon. We had four lessons each school day and attended school every day of the week except Sunday.

The school building was furnished with a stove, a blackboard and two rows of desks. The girls were told to sit together in one row, and the boys sat in the other row. Each desk had a small inkpot, but the students were required to bring their own ink. Most of the students did not have ink pens so the teacher handed out several pens that the students were to share. The points of the pens were made of iron and so our fingers and faces were always spotted with ink as we worked on our assignments. The teacher had only a small supply of paper; however, each student was given a notebook in which to do all of the class work. The teacher did not have enough textbooks for each student so a textbook was shared by several students. I would, for example, take home a textbook one day, and another student would take it home the following day. At home I completed my assignments using paper that my mother gave me. She worked in the administrative office of the collective farm and found the paper in the waste paper baskets.

I remember one old teacher who was very strict with us. She showed little sympathy toward me after I injured my hand during one of our breaks. It felt as if I had broken a bone, but she told me to write with the injured hand anyway. One of the boys in class tried to help me with my work, but when the teacher saw this she punished him. In our school a teacher used only one kind of punishment and that was to have a student stand in the corner of the classroom until the end of the lesson. When it was time to go home, I had great difficulty carrying my wooden box, which held my books and notebooks. I was sure that my hand was broken.

Throughout the school year the students participated in artistic activities. These activities included singing, dancing and reciting poetry. Many of the songs that were sung and poems that were recited were about the Motherland, Stalin and Communism. Special concerts were arranged for State holidays such as May 1, the anniversary of the October Revolution (November 7), the Soviet Army birthday (February 23), International Woman's Day (March 8), Victory Day (May 9), and New Years Day.

Of all the holidays, I liked New Years Day the most. About a week before New Years Day, a large pine tree was brought into the school building. On the following day, we would hang in the tree the decorations that we had made. These included small flags, paper chains and Chinese lanterns.

It was also traditional for a family to bring a pine tree into the house during New Years, and many people still do this in the village. The trees are usually acquired from a nearby forest in spite of the fact that cutting down trees is prohibited. In the recent past, people have been decorating their pine trees with small colored electric lights and small brightly colored toys. These items are now sold in the village store, but back when I was in elementary school toys and items such as chewing gum were not sold in the village.

There was a woman who made chewing gum. Her name was Anastasia Alemanova and I and other young people would often walk to Izmaelovka where she lived to purchase gum from her. She made it out of birch bark. She would gather large amounts of the bark from the nearby forest and boil it using two basins. Both basins contained water but the smaller basin in which she placed the pieces of bark was placed inside the larger one. The end product had a strong flavor, which was long lasting. We had no money with which to purchase the gum so we gave Anastasia a chicken egg for a piece of gum the size of a walnut. We then walked home with our prized possessions, and I would chew my piece whenever I worked on my school assignments at home.

Following my graduation, I and several other students in the village took an examination, which tested us on the Russian language, history and mathematics. The students who passed the examination were permitted to continue their education. If their parents wanted them to go on with their education, the students would be enrolled in the fifth grade in the school at Kizil.

In Kizil the village students rented rooms that were made available by resident families. My mother did not have the money to pay the rent for a room that I would need or even a mere corner in someone's house with a rug on which to sleep. Mother could not afford to buy me a winter coat or shoes that I would also need if I moved to Kizil. She told me that instead of going to the fifth grade, I would have to begin working. I was devastated and sat by the window and cried for a long time. I loved to study and had hoped one day to attend a university in a large city such as Moscow. I had often dreamed of becoming a scientist or a teacher or a manager of a state enterprise. These dreams came to an end.

My first job on the collective farm was taking care of more than forty calves. I was just eleven years old and legally not permitted to work, but the farm administrators changed the birth date on my documents making me fourteen years old. My responsibilities included feeding the calves, walking them and making sure that they did not wander off. I would wake up before sunrise and walk to the cow barn where the calves were kept in a fenced-in area next to the barn. The calves were no older than four months so I had to feed each calf three to four liters of milk from which much of the butterfat had been extracted. I had to make sure that each calf received its portion of milk.

I walked home to eat dinner at around noon but was back with my calves by 3:00 P.M. At that time I took the calves for another walk, and after we returned to the barn I gave each another meal consisting of milk without butter fat. A calf would stop receiving milk at the age of six months. It then began drinking water from a long log that had been hollowed out and made into a trough. I made sure that I followed carefully the directions that had been given to me. I did not want a single calf to die. "I wonder what the authorities would have done to me if a calf had died under my care."

Later on I worked as a pig tender. I arrived at the piggery early in the morning of each workday. My first task was to clean the pigs and their pens, and that was not easy. The suckling pigs had to be taken from their mothers and washed. When this was done, they looked like pink toys and were returned to their mothers. After cleaning the pigpens, I would give the pigs and piglets their food and water.

I became a milkmaid a year later. I was assigned to milk some twenty-five to thirty cows twice a day. It was hard work. When a cow gave birth, the milkmaid who was responsible for that cow was also responsible for the newborn calf. It was her job to feed the calf with milk from a bucket during the first two months of its life. It was the milkmaid that gave the calf its name, and every calf knew its mother-milkmaid.

One year I contracted brucellosis from an infected cow. At first I felt a terrible pain in my joints. The pain would travel from one joint to another. Eventually, I was brought to the hospital in Magnitogorsk. A kind doctor advised me to stay in the hospital until I was cured, but after I had been there for only a few days mother came to the hospital to ask me to return home because she needed my help in taking care of our house and the kitchen garden. The doctor said he could not prevent me from leaving the hospital but predicted that the illness would get worse and that I would be back under his care.

The doctor was right. Shortly after I returned home, I began to feel worse. I could not stand or sit. When I did lie down I felt a terrible pain throughout my body; I could hardly open my eyes or speak. I lay without moving, for the slightest movement was painful. It felt as if my head had been beaten by a hammer. My relatives finally transported me back to the hospital in Magnitogorsk. I do not know how I survived the trip.

Upon my return to the hospital, I became the patient of the doctor who had attended to me earlier. When he examined me he reminded me of his prediction. The doctor had been a military surgeon during the war and ordered that I be given a blood transfusion. He also prescribed milk injections. In three days I felt good enough to stand up, but I still had difficulty walking. I was given crutches; I would use them for a long time as I learned to walk again. I felt like a baby. Later, I was told that there were many people who suffered from brucellosis. Those who were given the milk injections recovered, but those who did not became paralyzed.

When I left the hospital to go home, the kind doctor jokingly promised that he would come to my wedding and dance with me if I should ever get married. I told him that I would be very glad to see him again. In time, when I did get married, God sent the kind doctor to my wedding feast. Apparently, he had visited a patient in the community of Yershovka, and on his way back to Magnitogorsk he passed through Zdanovka on the day of my wedding. When he asked the people of the village who it was that was being married, they gave him my name. He remembered my name and the promise that he made to me. When he entered the house where the wedding feast was being held I was surprised and happy to see him. He could stay for only a short time and then went on to Magnitogorsk.

Stealing was a common activity in our collective farm. It was particularly true in the years following the war when so many people suffered from food shortages. There was a young man with a wife and children who went into his neighbor's cellar to try to steal some sunflower oil. He was caught, but the neighbor did not report the incident. The man's attempt at theft was unusual because people would rarely steal from each other; they usually took items that belonged to the collective farm. I know there were milkmaids who would take home a pot of milk from the stockyard. People who were assigned to the farm piggery would take home fodder from the collective storage and feed it to their own pigs.

It was common for the village to be struck by natural disasters. There were spring seasons when the river bordering the village would rise and flood the land as the snows melted. If this occurred all the livestock owned by the collective farm was evacuated. The livestock that was owned privately was the concern of the owners. Many people would bring their calves and lambs to the tops of the heaps of manure that they had in their back yards. The manure was being saved by these people so that it could be made into bricks that would be used as fuel in the winter. After bringing the calves and lambs onto the heaps of manure, the owners would then bind together the legs of the small animals so that they could not move. When the water had risen high enough to flood the back yards of the village homes, the calves and lambs on the hills of manure remained untouched. In the meantime, the owners had taken their larger animals with them out of the village and out of harms way.

My uncle told me that he rescued a number of people and animals during the village floods. He was a tractor driver and, using his large tractor, he would rescue women and children and animals from houses that were flooded. He said that during one flood a woman who was in her eighties refused to leave her house because she would not leave her geese that were hatching their eggs in nests that she had made for them inside the house. My uncle tried to persuade her to come with him; she refused, and for two days she took refuge on top of her high Russian stove. Meanwhile the water inside had risen so high that the old woman's geese were swimming between the floating benches, brooms, table and bed.

Fires were also common in the village. If a fire broke out in a house, one of the neighbors would harness a horse and ride throughout the village shouting "Fire! Fire!" In other villages they had a large gong that would be struck to alert the people about a fire. Some villages used church bells to ring out the alarm. These bells had been taken from the churches that were dismantled at the time the villages were turned into collective farms. After the villagers were informed about a fire, they would come to the scene of the fire to put it out. If the burning house was located near the village river, the people formed a line from the river to the house passing from one person to another person buckets that had been filled in the river. The fire in a burning house located a far distance from the river was much more difficult to put out.

One evening my friend and I accidentally started a fire. I had invited my friend to the house and, because it was already dark outside, took out a kerosene lamp to light it. I was not aware that the lamp contained gasoline instead of kerosene. When I lighted the lamp, it seemed to explode. The table on which it stood and the floor below it as well as my fingers seemed to be on fire. I was terribly frightened, but my friend took her coat and covered the lamp and with it smothered the fire. The next day, as we went to school, our clothes and faces still bore the traces of the fire. For several years thereafter my girl friend continued to wear the blackened coat that she had used to save my house from fire.

If the manager of the collective farm asked for volunteers who were willing to do some additional work without pay, I would usually volunteer. For instance, one year the farm had an excess of wheat, which was left outdoors in large hills. When trucks were brought to the farm to bring the wheat to another location, I and some other girls volunteered to load the wheat onto the trucks. We worked all night loading the wheat onto the trucks. Young people were expected to contribute to the welfare of the collective farm by doing jobs for which they were to receive no compensation. We prepared, for example, the storage areas for the newly harvested grains, we cleaned the stockyard before the winter season, we plastered the buildings owned by the collective farm and we planted trees and grass in the village.

For my volunteer work and for my good job performance I was given bonuses and awards. The awards were usually gifts such as dresses or stockings. These items must have been purchased in Magnitogorsk or some other community because in the 1950s our village store did not sell them. I was thankful for the awards because I had neither the time nor the money to go to Magnitogorsk to buy these items

One year I was awarded the medal "For Valiant Labor." The work for which I received the medal was described in a newspaper distributed in Chelyabinsk. I was made aware of the award by my neighbor who showed me the newspaper. The medal was to be presented to me at the All-Union Exhibition of Developments of Economy of the USSR, which was to be held in Moscow. The administrators of the collective farm wanted me and some other girls to attend the exhibition as representatives of the farm; however, shortly before we were to leave for Moscow we were replaced by a delegation of men. I suspect that the Communist Party leadership on the regional level made that decision. Nevertheless, I did receive my medal.

It was years later when I attended an exhibition in Moscow. I and another woman were chosen by the farm administrators of Izmaelovka to represent Izmaelovka at the exhibition. We were to be members of a rather large delegation from the Chelyabinsk area. I had always dreamed of visiting Moscow, and I distinctly remember the trip. It was the first time in my life that I flew in an airplane. We departed from Magnitogorsk and arrived at the airport of Domodedova near Moscow. I watched with great interest the conveyor belt as it brought my luggage to me. I was fascinated with the people at the airport and recognized an old war veteran who I had seen on television several days before. From the airport, we were brought to a hotel. I remember thinking that only in Moscow does a person have such amazing experiences.

During our stay in Moscow we attended the exhibition and were taken on several excursions. The excursions included trips to the major museums of Moscow. We also visited Lenin's Mausoleum at Red Square. There were many people who had come to see Lenin, and we stood in line for several hours. I remember my knees trembled as I entered the mausoleum for I had been taught since childhood that Lenin was the greatest leader of the workers throughout the world. The walk through the mausoleum lasted only a few minutes, but it left a lasting impression on me. As a commemoration of the trip to Moscow and my participation in the exhibition, I was given a medal.

Stalin died on March 3, 1953. In the days previous to his death, mother and I would visit our neighbor's home every evening to listen to a radio receiving set. We would listen in deep silence to the report of Stalin's illness. When it was reported that he had died, we wept softly and wondered anxiously what would happen to us now that the father of our country was gone.

In order to earn extra money, mother knitted shawls made of goat's wool. Knitting a shawl was a long and extensive process. First, mother had to clean and then comb the white wool. Then, she spun the strands of wool into thread using a spinning wheel. Finally, she took the thread and, using two knitting needles, made a shawl. The knitting was done during the winter evenings in the dim light of a kerosene lamp or a candle. If she knitted for several hours each evening she would finish one shawl in a month. Mother would take her shawls, they were called Orenburg shawls, to Magnitogorsk in the spring, and there they would sell for as much as eighty rubles a piece. This was more than a teacher's monthly salary. One year, mother sold a shawl for such a high price that with the money she was able to buy me a gray colored suit and a wristwatch. It was wonderful. I never dreamed that I would own a suit or a wrist watch.

As I grew older, I developed a passion for social activities such as dancing. I often watched the older girls in the village dancing in the street. They would ask me to join them, but each time I refused. Eventually, the girls that were my age and I would meet in each other's homes and dance together. Sometimes we would stay up till midnight dancing. Whenever my friends came to my house to dance, mother would leave the house and visit a friend and take with her a shawl that she was knitting.

Later on the administration of the collective farm gave the young people an old granary to use as a Village Club. We repaired the granary in our spare time. It became the center of entertainment. In the new Village Club we arranged song festivals and dances. Someone who knew how to play an accordion would play at the dances, and the dances would last until midnight. We had no clock, but we could tell time by the crowing of the cocks. A cock crows as the sun begins to set. After that it falls asleep and will remain silent until midnight. When we heard a cock crowing at midnight, it meant that it was time to go home.

It was at a dance that I first saw my husband. His name was Michael. He had come to our village in 1955 with a Komsomol Pass from the secret town of Sim located in the Chelyabinsk region (see Glossary - Komsomol Pass). He was sent to our village as a tractor driver to cultivate the virgin steppes in our area. When he first started coming to our Village Club dances he preferred to dance with the older girls and not with me or my friends for we were much younger. In time, however, he made an effort to talk to me, and we became friends.

In 1956 Michael was drafted into the army. Before entering into the military, he asked me if I would wait for him. I asked him why, and he replied that we were friends. He wanted me to wait for him. I made no promises. I did agree to see him off. I also answered the letters that he sent to me during the first year of his military service. Thereafter, I did not answer his letters.

Michael returned to our village after his three years of military service were completed. I did not love him, and when he came to see me I greeted him in a cold manner in order to discourage him from wanting to see me again. He agreed to forget me and promised to move to another village. Apparently the people with whom he was staying had persuaded him to approach me again, and this time he asked me to be his wife. I said no.

The next morning, as I walked to work, Michael met me along the way and with him was the woman in whose house he was staying. Again he proposed to me. I became nervous. My tongue stuck to the roof of my mouth, and I could not answer. I tried to get away from them, but they insisted that I come with them to see my mother. My mother was home and had already prepared the table for guests to sit at. Mother and the other woman then had Michael and me stand next to each other on the same floorboard. They then asked Michael if he wanted to be Nina's husband. He answered yes. After that they asked me if I would like to be Michael's wife. I remained silent. In frustration, the two women told us to go for a walk and said that while we were gone they would arrange our marriage. Meanwhile, a friend who was also a milkmaid arrived at the house to tell me that I had to hurry or else we would be late for work. As she entered our house, she immediately recognized what was happening, and in no more than five minutes the entire village knew that Michael and I were to be married. Some of my friends came by and warned me not to marry Michael because they knew that he loved to drink. It was too late. My Mother had already spoken for me and had said that I would marry Michael.

Michael and I had the traditional three-day wedding feast. My mother's house was too small to accommodate the wedding guests and Michael had no house at all so an old woman volunteered to have the feast in her two room wooden house. Mother and I and some relatives prepared the food for the feast. Although we were poor, we were able to get together enough food. We prepared meat, which included chicken and geese, and we made pies and cakes and candies. Michael did not offer to help us with these preparations and neither did his relatives. In fact, his parents did not even come to the wedding.

The wedding assistants brought Michael and me to the wedding feast in a sleigh pulled by three decorated horses. As we entered the old woman's house, we were greeted by relatives and friends who congratulated us and drank to our health with small glasses of "kislushka." I was wearing a simple dress decorated with small flowers. I had no wedding dress, which was just as well since I had no love for the man I was marrying.

Shortly after we arrived at the feast, the bed "druzkas," a male and a female, told Michael and me to leave the feast and retire for the day in another house. I told them that I did not want to leave and began to weep. Nevertheless, they took me and brought us to our bedchamber. Then they locked the door and took the key as they left.

Early the next morning the bed "druzkas" returned and brought Michael and me to the second day feast. Shortly after our arrival, Michael began to drink. I did not like it. I did not like alcoholic drinks at all. Michael was raised in the city, and at that time the people in the cities drank much more than the people living in the villages. The adults in a village only drank on holidays. The young people never drank. As girls, we would entertain ourselves by getting together and knitting. When we got tired of that activity, we would put down our knitting and start singing and dancing. The young men of the village would entertain themselves with cards, and when they tired of that one of them would take up an accordion and play music. We had fun and did not need to drink alcohol in order to have a good time.

On the third day of the wedding, Michael drank again. I was repulsed by it. I was convinced that our marriage was a mistake; however, we remained married long enough to have three children.

My son Yergeny was born in 1960. There was no hospital in Zdanovka so I gave birth to my son at home with the assistance of an old experienced midwife. I had notified the woman of my pregnancy, and on the evening that I went into labor my mother went to get the old woman. The woman had already prepared a clean thread to tie the umbilical cord of the baby. She stayed with me all night long. She tried to help me in every way that she could. She had me do exercises, and then she had me lay next to the warm Russian stove. But I was unable to push my baby out. The old woman then told my mother to prepare a horse and cart and to take me to the hospital in Kizil. While the horse and cart were being made ready, the old woman tried one more method to get me to give birth. She had me put my long hair in my mouth to induce vomiting. The method was so disgusting that whenever I think about it I re-experience the taste of that hair. Nevertheless, it worked, and when my son was born the old woman washed him and then placed me and the infant on the warm Russian stove. I was so tired. The ordeal had started at 7 P.M. and ended at 8 A.M. the following morning. The old woman stayed with me that day and ordered my mother to heat the bathhouse. In the evening she took me and the baby to the bathhouse, and there she washed the baby again. She then placed the baby in my mother's arms and massaged my body for a long time.

The old woman would bathe my child and massage my body once a day during the next three days, and all of this was done without charge. Mother did feed the old woman while she stayed with us and prepared for her the best we had. Mother also gave her a gift. I do not remember what it was; it may have been some stockings or a piece of cloth, which could be made into a dress.

Natasha, my only daughter, was born the following year. Women were not given maternity leave at that time so on the third day after I gave birth to Natasha, I returned to my job. It was mother who cared for my baby and my one-year-old son.

I have only a few photographs of myself. I have no wedding pictures or pictures of my children as babies. The people of the village did not own cameras in the 1950s. The earliest photograph that I have of myself dates back to 1958. In that year a photographer from Magnitogorsk came to the village and took photographs of the people who wanted their picture taken. Many people had their picture taken, and I was one of them. It was an exciting occasion.

In 1962 we moved to Izmaelovka. My mother's sister and brother had lived in Izmaelovka for years, and after my aunt's husband died she invited us to come and be with her. We accepted the invitation, and upon our arrival were given by my mother's brother a small rather old house made out of the wood of larch trees. Houses like this were well constructed and would last for more than a hundred years. In one room of the house there were benches, a table, a Russian stove and a Holland stove. The second room, the living room, was furnished with a bed, a table and some chairs.

I do not know who constructed the house, but I am almost certain that the first owner with the help of his neighbors built it. They used to do that in villages on holidays. One neighbor would make the framework for the windows, another would plaster the walls and other neighbors would complete the other tasks. Later on, special teams of construction workers were organized who could be hired to build a house. These specialists would construct the foundation and the skeletal frame of the house. The remainder of the house would be built by the owner with the assistance of his neighbors.

The youngest of my three children was born in 1972. His name is Alexander, but I call him Sasha. As a child he, like my other two children, was well behaved. I rarely had to discipline my children, and only occasionally did I slap them as punishment. Each of them attended school, and each became a Young Pioneer and went several times to the Young Pioneers' camp held in Novinka. They enjoyed very much their experiences at the camp. Yergeny, my oldest son, moved to Magnitogorsk to attend a vocation school to learn to become a skilled construction worker. My daughter, Natasha, attended a vocation school as well and became a skilled plasterer and designer of mosaics. Sasha became a truck driver. He is still single. At the present time we are sharing the same dwelling place in Izmaelovka.

I never talked to my children about the meaning of life. I did not feel that this was necessary because in a Communist society the purpose of a person's life is obvious. We were expected to have at least an elementary education and then to work at some kind of vocation. We were told at village meetings that every human being should work as hard as possible for the welfare and future happiness of all the Soviet people. We were told to be good Communists, but I as well as most of the village people considered the Party's slogans mere empty words. The people who voiced these slogans at village meetings did not practice what they preached. Their actions betrayed them. They were more concerned about their own well-being than the welfare of others. I felt then and still believe today that a person's purpose in life is to give birth to life and then to nourish it. I have done that, and I am happy with my children. Inspite of the anti-religious policies that were enforced by the State for many years, I believe in God and live with the conviction that I am his adopted child.

After Sasha's birth, Michael and I separated from each other. When I inquired about getting a divorce, the authorities in Kizil told me that an application for divorce would cost me eight rubles. My monthly salary at that time was fifty rubles so to apply for a divorce was expensive. I was told that if I did apply for a divorce my husband and I would have to appear together before the regional People's Court. I did appear at the appointed time, but Michael did not. The clerks at the regional People's Court told me not to worry. They assured me that if I should ever desire to marry another man they would arrange, without Michael's approval, a divorce for me within two days. I have had no desire to marry again so technically I am not divorced. Yet everyone in the village considers me divorced.

During my early years in Izmaelovka, I worked as a milkmaid. The milkmaids were required to be at the barn early in the morning. I had no alarm clock, of course, so I accustomed myself to awaken with the cock's crow, which was around 5:00 A.M. Then I would get dressed and run to the barn without having breakfast or even a glass of tea. I was required to milk thirty cows before breakfast and this had to be done by hand; we had no electric milking machines. After completing that task, I gave the calves their milk and then cleaned the stockyard. When I finished the last task, I was permitted to go home and eat breakfast and shortly thereafter it was time to start milking another group of cows.

If a good movie was being shown at the Village Club house in the evening I would try to complete my duties at the stockyard as quickly as possible. The old clubhouse was too small to accommodate all of the people in the village so a person had to come early to get a seat. The showing of a movie was usually preceded by what was called a film magazine. A film magazine was a short newsreel that informed the people about the recent great successes of the Soviet Union such as the huge harvests.

As time went by, I stopped working as a milkmaid and was given a job working in the field. During the sowing season, I would have to get up early to deliver the seeds to the sowing machines before sunrise. The seeds had to be put in large boxes at the storage barn and then, using a cart pulled by a bull, I would bring the seeds to the field. It was so dark that I would not be able to see the road so I would simply direct the bull to the sound of the tractor that was plowing in the field. After the seeds were delivered, I had a couple of hours to feed my children and myself and work in our kitchen garden. Then I returned to the field and worked until evening.

When the sowing season was over the workers in the field were given a three-day vacation. On the first day the workers would come together and celebrate the completion of the sowing campaign. During the following two days the workers would work in their own kitchen gardens.

The field workers were given another three-day vacation after the crops were harvested. On the first day the people were entertained in the Village Club with a concert performed by musicians from Magnitogorsk who had been brought to the village for this special celebration. On the second day the people would gather along the far side of the village river and eat a meal of celebration. The people who were in charge of the village store would bring to the gathering beverages, alcoholic drinks, salamis, pies, candies and other treats. These were sold under the open sky. It was a nice gathering with people singing, dancing, telling jokes and laughing. The third day was a day of competitions, which included foot races.

There have been many difficult and many happy days in my life. The difficult times include the days when I had to get up early in the morning to work long hard hours. However, I try not to think about those times. I try instead to concentrate on the positive experiences in my life. Some of the most wonderful times took place in the Izmaelovka Village Club. Here I helped organize and prepare concerts with other women in the village. Wonderful personal relationships were developed at that time, and I had great fun singing and dancing.

Chapter Six

"War Widow and State Propagandist"

Anna Kostomarova (Khudiakova) and Valentina Nenasheva (Feodorova)

Anna was a young married woman when the Soviet Union was invaded in 1941. Her husband who was also Valentina's father had been drafted into the military a year before the invasion. He was killed near Budapest on January 27, 1945, shortly before the war came to an end. Anna grieved for many days, and in her state of grief she burned the letters that her husband had written to her. The body of Anna's husband was not returned to the Soviet Union and was probably buried in Hungary.

Anna would remarry after the war, and the second marriage was a disaster. She discovered shortly following the wedding that her husband was involved in an extra marital relationship. She forgave her husband for his unfaithfulness and became pregnant with his child. When she informed him about her condition, he told her the child could not be his. He insinuated that her pregnancy was the result of an illicit affair. Anna was so offended by his remarks that she ended her pregnancy with an abortion.

Anna's third marriage was to a man named Ivan. He was much older than Anna and had four children from a previous marriage. At the time that Anna began living with Ivan, he was not officially divorced, and he and Anna would not be married until after Anna gave birth to their son. Anna and Ivan loved each other very much and would remain together until Ivan's death. Ivan would be a good stepfather for Valentina, and she remembers him with great affection and respect.

Valentina came to Izmaelovka in 1957 after her stepfather was appointed chairman of the collective farm. Valentina was eighteen years old when her stepfather placed her in charge of Izmaelovka's Village Club. The Village Club served as a cinema, as a theater for concerts and plays and as a dance

Anna is the mother of Valentina and their life accounts have been combined.

78

hall. It was Valentina's responsibility to show the movies that the State sent to the village. She was also held responsible for organizing and directing the concerts and plays that were performed by the members of the farm. Although these forms of entertainment were not professional in quality, the people of the village attended the performances faithfully, listened to them attentively and applauded them heartily. The entertainment in the Village Club was a wonderful diversion from the hard work to which the members of the collective farm were subjected.

In 1959 Valentina became the village librarian. As the librarian she was to purchase books for the library with the money that was given to her by the authorities. She also received from the State newspapers that she was to make available to the villagers. The newspapers were organs of propaganda, and the leading articles were filled with slogans. According to Valentina, most of the villagers did not read the leading articles. They did not believe in the great accomplishments that the State proclaimed. They knew it was propaganda and felt that almost everything the State reported was a lie.

As the village librarian Valentina was required to inform the people of Izmaelovka about the State's policies. She did this by going out in the fields to where the workers were eating their afternoon meals and described and explained to them the State's new strategies. Most workers, Valentiana remembers, ignored her. The few people who did listen laughed at the information she was feeding them. Valentina also tried to communicate the information to audiences that attended the village concerts. She acted as the State's propagandist in Izmaelovka for more than thirty years. She knew that the information she conveyed was nonsense, but she did it to keep her job.

ANNA AND VALENTINA'S ACCOUNTS
ARE TOLD BY VALENTINA

My mother named me Valentina and gave birth to me while she and my father lived in Kazakhstan. My parents were married in Amour on the steppes of the Ural region, but in the spring that followed, they and my father's parents moved to a village located near Chimkent, a city in southern Kazakhstan. They believed that they would have a better life there because Kazakhstan offered a warm climate, good harvests and an abundance of fruits.

The village in Kazakhstan was a collective farm that specialized in the production of cotton. The farm needed laborers so my parents were given jobs upon their arrival. They were unfamiliar with cotton farming and discovered it was hard work. Mother and father and his parents purchased the remains of a broken down mud brick house, and together they repaired it. The repairs were made in their spare time, and it would take the entire summer to complete them. They also restored the kitchen garden, which came with the house.

In autumn my father received a physical examination notice from the medical commission of the Soviet military. Father traveled to Chimkent, passed the medical examination and was informed that he would be inducted into the military in several months. Father decided to stay in Chimkent and found a job working at the weigh scales at the railroad station. Soon thereafter mother joined him, and together they lived in an apartment in the city. They felt homesick for Amour and would return to their native village in August, which was when they were paid by the collective farm for the work they had done in the cotton fields.

I have no recollection of my father. I was just seven months old at the time my father was called into military service. He left in June 1940, a year before fascist Germany invaded the Soviet Union. Initially, father was stationed as a signal operator in Kandalaksha, which was not far from Leningrad. Many months later he wrote mother that his regiment was leaving the forests and marshes of Kandalaksha. He was happy about that because there were too many mosquitoes in the area. Father never came home from the war. When I visited my native village as a young girl, the people there recognized my father's features in me, and they remembered him as a personable and warm-hearted man. Their description is the image that I have of my father, and it is one that I treasure.

Mother learned about the start of the war on Sunday, June 22, 1941. She and her sister-in-law had just finished making manure fuel bricks and were at the village river washing their hands and feet. Suddenly on the other side of the river a man on horseback appeared who shouted that everyone was to go to a meeting that was to be held at the Village Council building. Mother had a feeling that the meeting was called to announce war. At the meeting the people of Amour were told that fascist Germany had attacked the Soviet Union along the western border and had bombed the western cities of the country.

In the days that followed the announcement, the people of Amour received many notices from the State. A number of men were called into the military and were told to report immediately. The village was ordered to send its horses to the State so that they could be used in the war effort. The young girls were told that they were to learn to drive tractors and operate combines so they could take the place of the men who had been drafted.

Mother and some other young women were sent to the Machine Tractor Station in Polotsk to study machines. The women were divided into two groups. Those who had never worked with a machine were taught to drive a tractor. The women who had observed the work done by a combine or who had worked as assistants to combine operators were taught to operate a combine. No one asked the women if they wanted to do so.

Mother was taught to drive a tractor. Her training began with a series of lectures given by the engineer at the Machine Tractor Station. He described, in detail, the parts of the machine and how they worked. The lectures were followed with lessons in driving a tractor. After a month of training, mother was declared qualified to drive and maintain a tractor.

Mother began working as an assistant to her brother, Pavel. My uncle was one of a small number of men who had been exempted from the military because he was an advanced tractor driver. He was a leading worker who received several medals of honor for his work. He also took part in the All-Union Agricultural Exhibition in Moscow.

As Uncle Pavel's assistant, mother maintained the tractor and the combine that they used. Periodically, she would use a long syringe to oil the gears of both machines. As the combine operator, she would pull and push levers that would raise and lower the knives that mowed the stalks of wheat. If a large stone was in the path of the combine the knives had to be raised in order to avoid their damage. The type of combine that was used was named "Stalinetz." With a "Stalinetz" a tractor driver and an assistant could reap some twenty hectares (50 acres) of wheat in one day. Uncle Pavel and mother were such hard workers that they would mow up to 100 hectares (250 acres) of wheat per day.

My uncle and mother were often sent to other collective farms that had difficulty harvesting their wheat. Tractor drivers and combine operators who worked with machines that belonged to a Machine Tractor Station received their work assignments from the station's director who in turn received his orders from the committee members of the regional Communist Party. If the committee was informed that a collective farm within their region was having difficulty harvesting its crop, they ordered the Machine Tractor Station director to send the best crew of tractor drivers and combine operators in the region to that farm. It was usually Uncle Pavel and his crew who were sent. They would work long days and sleep only two to three hours a day to get the job done.

In November they were sent to a collective farm named "Stalin's Way." There they lived at a work post consisting of two small dwellings. They worked all day long every day of the week below the hills that were already covered with snow. The combines had no booths so mother had to work under the open sky in the cold November wind. Of course she caught a cold, and her skin was covered with sores.

Eventually, mother became a tractor driver and was assigned a young boy to assist her. It was the boy's responsibility to make sure that mother's combine was functioning properly, but he was always getting into trouble. One day he climbed into the threshing box of the combine. When mother started up the tractor and put it into gear she heard a loud howl from inside the threshing box. She stopped the tractor immediately and found her young assistant hanging from the bars, which made up the framework of the box. If mother had not stopped, the boy's arms and legs would have been broken.

On another night mother was involved in an accident that could have scarred and disfigured her body. The engine of her tractor stalled in the field that she was plowing, and she could not get it started again. She walked in the dark to the field camp to get some benzene. At the camp she filled a pail with benzene, lighted a torch and then began her walk back to the tractor. What she did not notice was that her hand was wet with benzene. She was in a hurry, and in her haste she stumbled over a stone and fell to the ground with the torch in her hand. Her hand ignited, but mother calmly put her hand into the soft plowed soil and smothered the fire.

After the crops were harvested, mother was sent to Polotsk to work in the region's Machine Tractor Station. Each region had a Machine Tractor Station. A collective farm that used the tractors and other agricultural machines that the State had loaned to the Machine Tractor Station had to pay for their use. Payment was due at the end of a harvest season, and it was made by giving the State a percentage of the farm's harvest. The State's tractors and other machines were returned to the Machine Tractor Station so that they could be cleaned and repaired during the winter months. Mother and many other women from the collective farms throughout the region were assigned to work at the station in Polotsk the entire winter.

The women's work was supervised by Uncle Pavel and three other men. After cleaning the frame of the tractor, they removed the engine and transmission. The work was done outside in the snow and in thirty-degree weather. After loosening the nuts with tools, the women turned the nuts with their fingers. It was impossible to work with mittens, and many times mother's fingers would stick to the ice-cold iron. It was terrible work but the women had to do what they were told. When the engine and transmission were removed they were brought into the workshop of the Machine Tractor Station. Here they were repaired by the mechanic at the station. After the necessary repairs were made, the engine and transmission were reinstalled by the women.

Mother did not know of anyone becoming ill at the station. No one caught a cold in spite of the low winter temperatures. No one suffered a stomachache, which was truly amazing considering the women often drank polluted water. The water in the station was kept in an iron barrel, which had previously been used to transport oil. Thus, the surface of the water in the barrel was always covered with a thin layer of oil that had to be blown to the side gently before a person could get a drink.

Mother and eleven other women who worked at the station lived in a two-room house in Polotsk. The house was owned by an old woman who was living with her three grandchildren and a young Jewish woman who had been evacuated from European Russia. The old woman and the Jewish woman occupied the two beds, and the others slept on the floor.

In the evenings the women at the Machine Tractor Station would visit and sing songs. There was a radio receiving set in the main building of the station, and many evenings the women would go to the building and listen to the latest news about the war. After the broadcast they would talk about the war. They cursed Hitler and dreamed about a Soviet victory. Mother said that these shared experiences created among the women a bond of friendship.

Mother was permitted to go home once every two weeks. Upon her arrival, she would immediately go to the bathhouse to wash herself and her clothes that were saturated with machine oil. After washing her clothes, she would wait for them to dry. When they were dry she put them on and would not take them off again until after she returned to the bathhouse two weeks later.

During the second year of the war, mother was assigned to a brigade of twelve or more tractor drivers. They lived together in a wheeled building that was brought onto the field they were plowing. It was spring and inside the building it was uncomfortably warm, yet mother could not remove any of her clothes because the men in the brigade also slept in the building. There were no beds in the building so mother placed her coat on the floor and slept on that in her clothes.

One day at around dinnertime a military officer from Kizil arrived at the brigade camp. He joined the brigade workers as they sat down to eat. Mother had kitchen duty and noticed that the military officer was watching her as she served the food and mopped the floor near the washbasin. Later in the day, the military officer approached mother and asked her to marry him. He said he loved her and wanted to provide her with a good quiet life. Mother told him she could not marry him for she was already married and was waiting for her husband's return from the war. The military officer was the first of several men during the war that wanted to marry my mother.

One evening the brigade leader, mother and two other tractor drivers were supposed to drive two tractors from Amour to a nearby village. On the way they had to cross a river, but there was no bridge. Mother was sitting on the side of the tractor that was being driven by the brigade leader. As the tractor crossed the river, one of the wheels dropped into a hole. The jolt caused mother and a large empty milk churn to fall into the icy water. The brigade leader yelled at mother "Fedotova! Don't lose that milk churn!" Mother realized the brigade leader was more concerned about retrieving the milk churn than about her safety. She was so offended that she told him that he and the milk churn could go to hell. The brigade leader told Tonya, my mother's partner, to get the milk churn before it was carried away by the river. Tonya obeyed and barely got it in time. Meanwhile, mother had made her way to the riverbank and had driven the second tractor into the river in order to pull the first tractor out of the hole. The second tractor shut off because of the water, and now there were two tractors that needed to be rescued. The brigade leader ordered that mother and Tonya run to Amour to get a third tractor.

The run back to Amour was terrible. It was dark, and since it was early spring the low fields, which normally were covered with water in the summer, were covered with a thin layer of ice. As the two girls ran through these fields the ice cut and bloodied their legs, and the cold wind penetrated their clothes. When mother arrived home several hours later, my grandfather was astonished to see her and asked what had happened. Mother replied cynically that she had gone swimming and then proceeded to tell him the entire story. My grandfather was so angry that he cursed the war, he cursed Hitler, he cursed the brigade leader and he cursed the others that he held responsible for my mother's ordeal. Mother changed her clothes, found a third tractor and drove it to the river to rescue the other tractors.

During the war there was much hunger, and the women who worked in the fields would sometimes take home wheat to keep their children alive. Mother told me of two women whose husbands were at the front and whose children were near the point of starvation. These women winnowed several handfuls of wheat and took them home. What they did was considered a crime, and when they were caught they were tried by the regional People's Court in Kizil. The trial was held in the schoolhouse of Kizil. The women were declared guilty of stealing from the State, but they were not imprisoned. The people in charge of the trial realized that imprisoning the women would leave their children without anyone to care for them, and if that should happen the children would die. Instead the women were reprimanded severely and warned not to steal again. Throughout the reprimand, the authorities repeated again and again that most of the food produced by the farm was to be sent to the Soviet armies. It was, they said, the farm's contribution toward the war effort and they, the villagers, would have to do with less. Mother said the authorities expected the people to accept without question anything the State decided. The people were not to think for themselves. They were supposed to obey the orders of those who were above them.

The person who did challenge a superior could suffer serious consequences. Mother remembered this happening to an elderly man in Amour. The old man had been ordered by his brigade leader to work at a task that the old man believed he was unable to do. He asked the brigade leader to appoint a younger man to do it, but the brigade leader insisted that he do it. The old man then threatened to blackmail the brigade leader. In the past the brigade leader had sent trucks filled with wheat to the city of Chelyabinsk. The money that was made from the sale of the wheat was pocketed by the brigade leader. The old man was aware of this and threatened to tell the village about it if the brigade leader forced him to do the task. The brigade leader yielded, but several days later he sent the old man on an errand to the forest with a horse and cart. When the old man entered the forest, he was met by two men who had been hired to kill him. They grabbed the old man and murdered him; they then tied the horse to a tree. When the old man did not return to the village, a search was initiated. The search lasted almost a week and ended when the old man's body was found. The horse tied to the tree was also found. The animal, weak from hunger, had great difficulty standing. It had eaten off all the bark that it could reach on the tree. The brigade leader was questioned about the murder of the old man and was brought to trial. He did not implicate the killers that he had hired but instead confessed that he had murdered the old man. As a consequence, the brigade leader was sentenced to eight years in prison.

What I remember most about the war years is that there were ten of us living in one house. There were my gandparents, Uncle Pavel and his wife and two sons, my two aunts and mother and me. Since Uncle Pavel and mother worked and slept out in the fields, we rarely saw them. It was my grandmother, Maria Luckjanovna, who took care of the house and watched over me and my two cousins. I called my grandmother "granny."

My grandparents' house had an enclosed porch, a small storage room near the entrance door and two large rooms. The small storage room housed a wooden box in which we kept our flour. The first large room was both a kitchen and dining area. It was furnished with a table and some chairs and benches. Near the benches we had our "Red Corner," the place where granny had hung the family's icons and icon lamp. These were covered by a curtain, and only during a time of worship would they be uncovered. Near the door, which led to the living room, was a wooden bed, and several feet above the bed was a wooden shelf that had been built into the wall. The shelf was also used as a bed. In order to get to the shelf a person had to climb to the top of the Russian stove located next to the bed and then slide onto the shelf. The stove was part of the wall, which separated the two large rooms so that the stove would provide both rooms with heat. In the living room, the other large room, there were two more beds, a table, a chest of drawers and a trunk. On the walls were photographs and some hangings made of calico printed with patterns. The windows were covered with curtains made of gauze-like cotton.

The house had a flat roof, and during the hot summer nights the members of the family would sleep on the roof. In the backyard we had a kitchen garden and our outdoor toilet.

When the weather turned cold the Russian stove was used as a bed. It was around six feet high and at the top there was a place for sitting or lying down. To reach the top a person had to place one foot in a special step that had been built into the stove. In the morning when a fire was burning in the stove its top was hot to the touch, but in the evening when the stove was filled with smoldering embers the top of the stove was warm. Covering the top of the stove were some pelts or a mattress on which a person could sleep, and I would often sleep on the stove on cold nights. It was warm and comfortable.

Before taking me to bed, granny would check my hair for lice and at the same time tell me a story. Sometimes the story was about my father, but more often it was a fairy tale. Usually the fairy tale involved witches or goblins. One story was about a witch who lived in our village a long time ago. The witch turned herself into a pig one day and ran through the streets of the village. Someone caught the pig and cut off its ear. When the witch turned herself into a human being again she was missing one of her ears, and that is why she always wore a shawl over her head.

Granny never told me stories about soldiers at war. I thought this was odd since my father was fighting against the Germans. I discovered later that to say anything negative about the Soviet war effort was forbidden. One was not to talk about the increasing number of Soviet soldiers who were losing their lives. I guess granny considered it unwise to discuss the war with me because if I repeated what she had said to others they might interpret her comments as criticisms of the Soviet war effort.

It was granny who prepared the family's meals. She would start a fire in the stove early in the morning usually at around 4:00 A.M. or 5:00 A.M. After the fire had burned out, she would move aside the hot embers so that she could bake the bread. She had prepared the dough the previous day and had kept it in a wooden tub. She took the risen dough and divided it into manageable lumps and placed each one in the stove on top of a cabbage leaf. When the rounded loaves were baked, granny would splash the top of each one with water in order to make the crust soft.

It was difficult to feed a large family, but granny did the best with what she had. Most of the meals were made with food we grew in our kitchen garden. When granny made cabbage soup, she took potatoes, cabbage, carrots, beets and some dill and salt and placed these ingredients in a cast-iron kettle filled with water. She then put the kettle in the stove and left it there for several hours. Granny would also boil potatoes that were unpeeled. Thereafter, she would peel them, place them in a frying pan and bake them in the stove.

When they were ready to be eaten, granny would sprinkle them with salt and horseradish. The baked potatoes were delicious. Sometimes, granny would put an entire pumpkin in the stove or she would place pieces of pumpkin in the kettle and cook them for several hours. The pumpkin was deliciously sweet. We had no sugar at this time so pumpkins were a special treat.

In the summer the family would eat outside. I remember we would sit in the backyard and gather around the samovar. While the water in the samovar was being heated, we would eat "zatiruka." It is a soup that is made with potatoes and flour. When it is ready to be served, some leek or some other grasses may be added. It was delicious, and I still enjoy it. After we finished our soup, we drank some tea made with sage and the heated water from the samovar. We would add to the tea fresh non-pasteurized milk from our own cow.

We ate better in the summer than in the other seasons. In the summer we would go into the open field and gather many wild grasses such as leek and garlic. We also gathered cabbage and field mushrooms. Granny would take the mushrooms and fry them in butter or she would add them to soups. All the wild plants, if prepared properly, were delicious. We also picked lots of strawberries and cherries that grew wild. A portion of the strawberries were dried for the winter so that they could be used as fillings in pies or dumplings.

In preparation for the winter granny would pickle cabbage. The cabbage was first chopped up in a large tub, and then it was placed in layers in a wooden barrel. Granny would first put down a layer of chopped cabbage, and then she would add some sliced carrots and dill. These would be covered by leaves of cabbage. Then she would repeat the process by placing on top of the leaves another layer of chopped cabbage and still more sliced carrots and dill until the barrel was full. Later this pickled cabbage was used in a potato meal with maybe some meat. In another barrel granny pickled cabbage with chopped beet roots which were used to make beet root soup called borsch.

Granny also pickled mushrooms. The mushrooms were white in color and were gathered from a nearby forest. The mushrooms were so numerous in the forest that in an afternoon we could fill a horse-drawn wagon. The first step in preparing mushrooms for pickling was to soak them in water overnight in large wooden tubs. The following morning, the mushrooms were cleaned by wiping them with grasses. They were then placed in small birch bark barrels with salt and spice, and finally the barrels were stored in our cellar where they would remain cool.

I loved my grandmother and followed her wherever she went. If, for example, she walked to the backyard to our outdoor toilet I would be behind her. Then she would turn around and say "Valya, leave me alone for a few minutes." She never punished me. It was she who raised me for I rarely saw my mother. It was not my mother's fault. She would have preferred staying home with me instead of working and sleeping at the Machine Tractor Station in the winter and in the fields during the other seasons of the year. When mother was permitted to come home, which was one day out of every two weeks, granny would push me toward her and say, "Look, there is your mother. Go to her and let me relax for a while."

By observing my grandmother I learned to be a good homemaker. She taught me how to take care of houseplants, to plant and care for a productive kitchen garden, to cook delicious meals and to wash floors and clothes. I used to watch her prepare an alkaline solution that she would use to wash clothes. She would take the ashes out of the stove and drop them into boiling water in a wooden washtub. After the pieces of ash had settled to the bottom she would stick a special washboard in the tub and use that to wash our clothes. Granny did not iron clothes because irons were not sold in the stores until the 1950s. Granny instead pressed our clothes by rolling them with a special wooden implement.

The hardships and deaths caused by war were nothing new to my granny. She had lost her first husband, a Cossack by the name of Gregory Salov, shortly after he returned from World War One. They had a son, my Uncle Pavel, who she had to raise. To help her with this responsibility, granny married my grandfather who had lost his first wife who had borne him four children. Granny and my grandfather were married in 1920. Following this union, one of my grandfather's sons was killed in the Civil War.

Death struck our family again in 1943. In that year the family received a vikluchka. I was four years old and sitting on our stove to keep warm as I listened to the family talk about the official correspondence. Granny had told me much earlier that my father was drafted when I was just a baby so I assumed the vikluchka announced my father's death. When I asked granny if it was my father who had been killed she looked at me in anger and replied, "Let God send a boil on your tongue for saying such a thing! Who told you this?" I was then told that the vikluchka was an announcement of my Uncle Jacob's death.

The vikluchka reporting my father's death came two years later. News of his death came as a shock, and I remember sitting on the stove and just crying. It was a shock because I was expecting his return. Everybody told me that the war would soon be over. The vikluchka said that my father was killed near Budapest on January 27, 1945. His body was not returned home, and I have never seen his grave site. I have asked other people who traveled to Hungary to look for his burial site, but none of them found it.

Mother grieved over father's death for many days, and in her state of grief she burned the letters that he had written to her. She had kept the letters in a large trunk. She did not save a single letter, and I never had the opportunity to read them. I saw father's handwriting only on his photograph on which he had written, "To my lovely wife and daughter, Velachka." Granny told me that in the letters that father wrote to my mother he had expressed a strong desire to see me even if it meant viewing me from a distance through a tiny crack in a wall. He also asked granny and my grandfather to help my mother raise his daughter while he was away.

Mother did not rejoice when it was announced that the war was over. She and the other young women in the tractor brigade learned of its end one evening upon their return to their wheeled dwelling after having worked in the field all day. Most of the young women were not married and they expressed their joy by laughing, jumping up and down, clapping their hands and embracing each other. Mother and another tractor driver who had also lost her husband during the war left the happy group to be alone because they did not want to be seen crying. These two young women would not be welcoming home their husbands. Mother loved my father very much and with his death she felt her life of happiness had come to an end.

Toward the start of 1946 mother met a handsome young man named Michael who had just returned from the war. They were married, but early in the marriage mother suspected that he was being unfaithful to her. There were certain developments that raised her suspicions. Michael was bringing lice into their bed, and mother suspected that they came from another woman. Michael would leave in the evenings and would not return home until late at night. Mother would ask him where he had been, and he would say that he had been visiting a relative to discuss his future employment. Then one evening they attended a party. Mother left the gathering to get something from home, and when she returned she found her husband in a shed making love to another woman. Mother should have left Michael, but she forgave him hoping that he would change.

Mother believed that her husband would settle down after she became pregnant. When she told Michael about her condition he replied that the child was not his. He said that because of a war injury it was impossible for him to produce offspring. He implied that mother had been involved in an illicit affair. Mother was so offended by his remarks that she decided to get an abortion; she did not want to give birth to Michael's child.

The abortion was performed by the village doctor's assistant. During the operation mother lost a large quantity of blood, and as she left the doctor's office she became dizzy and fell to the ground. She needed tender loving care and so she made her way to my grandmother's house.

Mother would speak to her husband several days later. They happened to meet in the street, and he asked her to come home with him. She told him then that she never wanted to see him again. Mother knew that he would not change and would continue having extra marital affairs. She knew the marriage was over and so they parted.

In the weeks that followed, Michael would harass mother. First, he submitted to the authorities a written statement accusing mother of ending her pregnancy with an abortion. It was illegal to perform abortions and the doctor's assistant who had performed the operation could have been imprisoned for what he had done. Finally, Michael began stalking mother. He warned her that if she did not return to him he would kill her. Michael stalked mother for more than a month.

Following the war, granny told mother to stop working for the farm so she could help her with the work at home. Taking care of me and the family cow and sheep and the kitchen garden had become too much of a burden for granny. Mother agreed and asked the chairman of the collective farm to permit her to quit the tractor brigade. He said that quitting was impossible because the collective farm needed my mother's labor. He did promise mother that there would come a time when her job responsibilities to the farm would end. Mother continued working for the farm another full year. Finally, in the fall of 1946, mother was released from the tractor brigade, and for the first time since the beginning of the war she was allowed to stay home.

Mother met the man who would become my stepfather on a trip to Polotsk. She went by horse and cart, and before she left she stopped at my uncle's house to say hello to him and his wife. After she tethered her horse and began walking to the house, she was greeted by her sister-in-law who told mother that the chairman of the collective farm, Ivan Kostomarov, was inside visiting with Uncle Pavel. She warned mother that the chairman was interested in her and would probably ask to marry her. Mother was shocked and told her sister-in-law to discourage Ivan from approaching her. Mother said that she had not recovered from her last marriage, a marriage that lasted only eight months. She told her sister-in-law that she did not want to go through that kind of hell again. Mother knew that Ivan was a married man and that he had older children, but later in the evening Ivan approached mother and asked her to be his wife. Mother told him that she could not talk about matrimony; she said she was still recovering from a terrible marriage and did not want to try her luck at marriage again.

After mother returned home from Polotsk, she told granny about Ivan and the proposal. Granny urged mother to reject the proposal reminding her that Ivan was married and had a family and was an older man. Mother informed granny that Ivan's marriage was over. He and his wife were no longer living together and would soon be officially divorced. Mother further pointed out that it was not necessary for a husband and wife to be close in age in order to have a successful marriage. She argued that she and her second husband had been close in age yet their marriage had been a disaster. "Maybe," she said, "it would be good to marry a middle-aged man." Mother discussed Ivan's proposal with Uncle Pavel sometime later, but he told her that he could not advise her on what to do. She would have to decide what was best. Mother made her decision by moving in with Ivan.

Mother and Ivan would not be married until much later. It happened after mother gave birth to their son in 1950. The State required that each newborn child be registered, and since mother was still not officially married her son would have to be registered as the offspring of a single mother. Ivan would not permit that so he made his marriage to mother official. The two loved each other very much and remained together until my stepfather's death. Ivan died at the age of seventy-one.

In 1947 Ivan was appointed chairman of a collective farm named Kazbakh, and it was here that I attended elementary school. Kazbakh was a poor farm; we saw nothing but poverty all around us. There were about thirty pupils in my class and I discovered that only two of them had fathers who were alive. The majority of the men on the collective farm had died during the war. My classmates were always hungry, even those who had fathers. One of them was my girl friend. I remember that her mother would tell her to bring food to her father who was working in the field. The mother gave her the food in a bag that she had sewn together so that her daughter would not be able to take and eat the food meant for her father.

In school I was taught that Stalin was a great man and leader. I believed what my teachers said, and as a result I thought Stalin was like God. The teachers noticed that I was able to memorize and recite poetry well and so on revolutionary holidays such as the first of May, the seventh of November and the fifth of December, they would have me recite poems, which described the greatness of Stalin. I believed sincerely the content of those poems. There were some students who disliked school and did not want to learn, but even these students accepted without hesitation that which was taught about Stalin.

There was a Young Pioneers' camp near Kazbakh, and the Young Pioneers throughout the region would come to this camp during the summer vacations. I and others my age would visit the campsite and watch from a distance the day's activities. In the morning the Young Pioneers would form a line near the camp flagpole, and one of them would raise a red flag. Later, a campfire would be built, and the Young Pioneers would seat themselves around it and sing songs. The songs were usually about Lenin and Stalin and about the happy life that a child enjoyed in the Soviet Union. When it was time for me to go home, I would hurry because I wanted to tell mother about all the fascinating events that I had witnessed at the Young Pioneers' camp. I longed for the day when I would become a Young Pioneer.

Almost every child became a Young Pioneer. I became a member of the Young Pioneers organization when I was in third grade. I remember with fondness the day that I was inducted. It was a grand ceremony. All the Young Pioneers of the school formed a line as they stood next to each other. Then with the sound of a Young Pioneers' horn and drum the Young Pioneers' banner was carried into the room. As I and the other candidates stood in front of the line of Young Pioneers, we took the ceremonial oath, which was to be faithful to the ideals of Communism. After that the oldest members of the Young Pioneers placed the traditional red ties around our necks. I was proud to be a member (see Glossary — Young Pioneers).

The Young Pioneers sponsored a number of activities. We had our own newspaper. We organized competitions. One competition involved our work at the school's kitchen garden. The Young Pioneers were divided into groups, and each group was assigned its own vegetable plot. After a while the group with the best plot was awarded a small red flag that was set up in the plot. The Young Pioneers also prepared concerts, which were given at the school on revolutionary holidays. Most of the songs that were sung at these concerts glorified Lenin, Stalin and Communism. The Young Pioneers also staged plays. We acted out, for example, the life of Zoya Kosmodeniankaja.

Zoya was a young Soviet female partisan in the war against the fascist Germans who had invaded our country. She carried out scorched earth tactics which involved burning anything that might be of service to the invaders. One day she was caught trying to set fire to some horse stables used by the enemy. The Germans tortured her and then hanged her. Zoya's body was found on a gallows west of Moscow in December 1941 during the Soviet Union's first successful counter attack in the war. She personified the country's fight against Germany.

One day my stepfather told my mother that he feared for his life. He had recently returned from Kizil where he had attended a closed meeting of the district committee of the Communist Party. During the meeting my stepfather and others discussed a disagreement that had developed between Stalin and Malenkov. After my stepfather told mother about the disagreement he became anxious for he feared that mother would talk to others about this problem within the nation's Communist Party. My stepfather feared that if the authorities discovered that he had shared this information with my mother he would be arrested. He went so far as to take out his gun to shoot himself. He told mother it was better to commit suicide than to be arrested by the NKVD. Mother promised him that she would tell no one about their conversation and finally persuaded him to go to bed. During Stalin's years of rule people like my parents lived in fear.

For my mother the most meaningful political change was de-Stalinization. Mother had always believed in the good intentions of Stalin and became deeply concerned for our country's future when she learned about his death. When Nikita Khrushchev came to power he exposed the people to Stalin's acts of cruelty and his policies of repression (see Glossary - Khrushchev's speech to the Twentieth Century Congress). Khrushchev also released thousands of people who were being held in prisons. As a result, mother and many others like her lived in less fear.

At the age of thirteen I joined the Komsomol organization as an exemplary Young Pioneer. Before I could be invited to be a member, I had to demonstrate that I knew the history of the Komsomol, that I was familiar with the Soviet Union's foreign policies, that I was knowledgeable about the accomplishments of the state farm in which I lived and that I could identify the farm's best workers. There were other requirements as well. As a member of the Komsomol I was asked many times to volunteer for a working assignment on the farm. I never rejected the requested volunteer work because to do so would have been dishonorable. I tried diligently to be a good Komsomol member (see Glossary—Komsomol).

In order to continue my education I had to attend the school in Kizil. I entered the eighth grade there and received a well-rounded education. I was taught sports and given military training. I took courses in mathematics, physics, chemistry, biology, geography, government, literature, history and the German language. Studying the German language was unpopular with most of the students.

The history teacher was also the principal of the school. He was a polite and soft natured man, and all the students respected him. He was a war veteran, but he never talked about his experiences as a soldier. He did not talk about Stalin's acts of repression during the 1930s. He did not mention that the Soviet Union had signed an agreement (non-aggression pact) with fascist Germany in 1939 nor did he talk about our country's military invasions of Poland, the Baltic republics and Finland. I suspect that these were forbidden topics. I did not learn about these events in our country's history until the 1980s when Mikhail Gorbachev was leading the country.

The school in Kizil had a library with a good collection of books, and I would visit the library often. My interest in reading began when I read Aladdin's Magic Lamp. The book was so interesting that I could not put it down. After that I read many adventure novels. My favorite authors of these novels were Jules Verne and Sir Walter Scott. I would also read the Russian classics and Leo Tolstoy was one of my favorite writers. I read Anna Karenina, and I remember my stepfather taking the book away from me because he felt that I was too young to be reading that kind of literature. Nevertheless, I finished it.

I also liked drama and at the school in Kizil I joined the drama club. I spent many hours reading plays and preparing for my parts in those plays.

My dream was to become a teacher in the middle grades or in the upper grades. I tried to pursue that goal after finishing my ten years of schooling. I traveled to Magnitogorsk in hopes of gaining admission into a school that prepared teachers, but the directors of the school informed me that they were only accepting people who wanted to become kindergarten teachers. Teaching kindergarten children did not appeal to me so I returned home. My dream would not come true. Our country is a land of people with broken dreams.

In 1957 my stepfather was appointed chairman of the Izmaelovka collective farm. Upon our arrival in Izmaelovka, I was asked by my stepfather to work at the village library. The job in the library was appealing, and I told my stepfather that I would take it. On the morning that I was to start my new job, a young lady with an education in library work arrived in the village, and she became the librarian.

My stepfather then placed me in charge of the Village Club. The building was a small wooden house without windows. There was a stove inside but nothing more. There were no benches or chairs. I was told that whenever a movie was shown by the previous people in charge of the Village Club, it was shown outside on the grass. I wanted to change that and turn the Village Club into a small cinema with benches on which people could sit.

The Village Club also served as a theater for concerts and plays, but in order to have concerts and plays I needed performers. I went throughout the community recruiting young women and men and organizing them into groups of singers, reciters, actresses and actors. There were times when it was difficult to bring together all of the participants to prepare a play. Sometimes the participants, having worked all day, were too tired to come to the Village Club and practice. Those of us who did show up would usually spend the entire evening together. When it was time to leave, we would walk home together singing songs. Singing is a strong tradition in Izmaelovka.

In Izmaelovka the people loved to come to the Village Club to attend a concert. Here they experienced an activity outside of the home other than work. Here they were entertained. Although the concerts were not professional in quality, the people listened attentively and applauded heartily. They would weep, and they would laugh for joy. The village people wanted to and needed to enjoy life as much as anyone. It was not their fault that they were born in a country that was misdirected by the Communist Party.

As the elected leader of the Komsomol organization in Izmaelovka, it was my responsibility to organize volunteer work projects for the membership. One of our projects was cleaning the wheat seeds that were to be placed in the village storage. It was a project that the Komsomol members had agreed to do. The work involved filling a barrel shaped container and rotating it with a handle. It was hard and dusty work, and we received no money for doing it. Volunteerism was our contribution to the collective farm.

Whenever the members of the Komsomol organization worked together we would discuss what we considered to be problems within the collective farm. We talked about the conduct of our friends. We discussed the directors of the farm and their relations with the workers. We all agreed that there were some people on the farm who worked hard yet they received less than others who did not put forth as much effort at their jobs.

What the farm did with Nickolai Firsonovich Alexmanov is a good example. Nikolai had been declared "Hero of Socialist Labor." He was given that title by the directors of the farm after the authorities in Kizil ordered them to choose a hero of labor for Izmaelovka. After Nikolai was chosen, the directors of the farm gave him credit on paper for plowing hectares of land that had been plowed by other workers. What they had done was lie and steal. The people on the farm eventually noticed what was being done, and they hated it. They lost respect for Nikolai and often upon seeing him they would say to each other cynically, "Look, there walks our hero." However, during the village meetings Nikolai was always mentioned as the best worker on the farm. He was glorified, and our "hero" liked the glory that was being bestowed upon him. He would go to the village school and give speeches telling the children about his job and the future plans for the farm. He would urge the school children to study hard and become good workers for the farm. I am not saying that Nikolai did not do good work. He was a good worker, but his brother, Alexander, was a better worker. Alexander, however, liked to drink vodka and was not a good speaker so the directors chose as the farm's "Hero of Socialist Labor" Nikolai who did not drink and who loved to address an audience (see Glossary—Hero of Socialist Labor).

Looking back, I do not believe anyone respected the so-called "Heroes of Socialist Labor." Most people worked hard and tried to do their best, and they felt that they too deserved a medal for their labors. Why then choose only one person to be given the title "Hero of Socialist Labor?" It was an injustice. The people viewed those who were declared heroes as boot lickers. I repeat, they did not respect these people.

It was easy to receive Komsomol membership but difficult to become a member of the Communist Party. I did not desire to become a Party member and never did, but one of my friends did seek membership. In an attempt to gain membership she participated in all of the Komsomol events. She studied and learned the history of the Communist Party and its policies. She fulfilled all of the Party's requirements, yet each time she applied for membership, and she applied several times, her application for admission was rejected. My friend was very straightforward and blunt, and I suspect that the Party leaders did not like that. She was very disappointed with each rejection and wept bitterly.

The procedure for becoming a member of the Communist Party was long. First the person seeking membership had to acquire letters of recommendation from three Party members. These letters along with a completed application had to be submitted to the Party's local organization. The directing committee of the local organization would review the letters and application and decide whether or not the applicant should be given a hearing. If they decided to give the applicant a hearing, the person would be brought before all the members of the Party's local organization. They would ask the applicant many questions. The questions concerned the history of the Communist Party, its rules and its programs and policies. If the answers to the questions pleased the local membership, the applicant was invited into the local membership. Thereafter, the directing committee of the Party's regional organization was informed about the decision made by the local organization. The regional committee checked the procedures used by the local organization, and if everything had been done in a satisfactory manner the applicant was given probationary membership status for one year. Following that year, the members of the local organization would consider the candidate's application once more. They reviewed the candidate's behavior and activities during the past year, both at work and at home. If the local organization decided that the candidate's membership was justified then the directing committee of the regional organization was informed. The committee would confirm the candidate's membership but only after the procedures used by the local organization had been verified.

In the 1950s the State expected the village workers to feed the nation's population but in turn left the villagers with barely enough for their own needs. It was the farm workers who plowed the dirt, planted the seeds, inhaled the dust and worked the long hours almost every day. What did they get for their labors? They certainly did not receive enough bread. Yet in the stores in Magnitogorsk there was an abundance of bread and different kinds of bread. The bread was also less expensive in the city than in the village. The bread that we bought in Izmaelovka was baked in Kizil, and the quality was inferior. If the people in the village learned that the village store had received some goods that were usually sold only in the cities, the people flocked to the store and formed a long line. I remember the times when I would stand in line for hours to buy those goods.

In 1959 I became the village librarian. The young lady who had been sent to the village to be our librarian two years earlier had left. I liked being a librarian. I would advise the people who came to the library on what to read. I arranged lectures on newly published books and on Russian and Soviet authors. I traveled often to the bookstores in Kizil and Magnitogorsk to purchase new books for the library. The Village Council paid for those trips, and the money used to purchase the books came from the cultural department of the regional administration board. They provided me with enough money to buy fifteen to twenty new books every month. The library also received each month a number of books from the State. However, about ninety percent of these books were political or were about agriculture, and virtually no one in the village showed an interest in them. The remaining books were Russian classics and children's stories. The classics included the writings of Alexander Pushkin, Mikhail Lermontov, Ivan Turgenev and Leo Tolstoy. The children's books were very good, and it was impossible to find these books in the stores.

It was from the magazines sent to the library that I learned about the crimes of Stalin. I read that before the war Stalin executed the most capable Soviet military officers and as a consequence when the German forces invaded our country the Soviet army was unable to stop the invasion. As a further consequence, millions of Russian soldiers and civilians lost their lives, and Stalin was the cause of their deaths (see Glossary-Khrushchev's speech to the Twentieth Century Congress).

I was shocked by what I read and decided that I should inform the people in the village about the newly published facts. With that in mind, I organized a special gathering just before Victory Day, May the ninth. I began the meeting by telling the people about the crimes of Stalin. Some of the veterans became outraged with my comments and began yelling at me. "Who gives you the right," they demanded, "to judge our great leader?" "Where did you get this information?" "What you are saying is a lie!" I responded by explaining that renowned Soviet historians had recently discovered secret documents in archives and that from these documents they acquired this information. These historians, I told them, concluded that the great human sacrifice suffered by the Soviet Union during the war could have been avoided. I told them that my father who fought against the Germans and was killed as a soldier gave me the right to judge Stalin. "If Stalin had not executed the most capable Soviet military officers my father might still be alive," I told them. What I said quieted the angry veterans. Later I was advised by other veterans, those who had supported me at the meeting, that in the future I should approach the subject of Stalin's crimes with greater finesse and diplomacy.

The library also received a varied selection of newspapers. The selection included "Pravda," "Proceedings," "Komsomol's Pravda," "Pioneer's Pravda," "Literature News," "New Books Review," a regional newspaper titled "For Communism" and some others. Most people did not read the leading articles in the newspapers because the articles were full of the State's slogans. The people simply did not believe the information put out by the State. They did not believe in the "great successes of the Soviet Union" proclaimed by the State's leaders. The villagers knew it was propaganda and nothing more. They were accustomed to thinking that most everything the State wrote and almost everything that was reported on the radio was a lie.

As the village librarian I was ordered by the District Committee of the Communist Party to inform the people on the farm about the new policies designed by the Central Committee of the Communist Party. I was told that I should do this out in the fields while the workers were eating their afternoon meal. I did as I was told, but whenever I explained the State's new strategies, most of the workers ignored me. They slept or talked to each other. The few workers who did listen to me laughed at the information that I was feeding them. However, as the State's propagandist on the farm it was my responsibility to expose the villagers to the State's policies. In time I developed a strategy to accomplish this.

I would organize periodically a concert at the Village Club. The people loved concerts and would attend them faithfully. Before the concert began, I would read the State's new policies and tell the village audience that life for the Soviet people was improving each day. I used this strategy in communication for more than thirty years. Looking back on those years, I am appalled at the kind of nonsense that I told the people. Yet I did it in order to keep my job.

Each month the people on the farm were exposed to a new slogan, which had been decided upon by the Communist leadership of the Soviet Union. One slogan read, "The economy must be economical." The slogan like so many other slogans was absolute nonsense. It was my responsibility to get the slogans painted on the posters or placards that were to be displayed in public places on the farm. These slogans kept our village painter busy, sometimes day and night. They were displayed, but few people took them seriously.

There were elections, but the people's votes meant nothing. It was the directing committee of the regional Communist Party that organized an election. The directing committee of the village Communist Party appointed a special elections commission to conduct the village election. The commission was to inform the people in the village about the candidates that were running for election. The commission also had to make sure that all the people voted on election day. On that day the people went to a collective farm administrative office to vote. The commission members were there to greet the voters and to give each an election ballot with the names of the candidates printed on it. All the candidates were members of the Communist Party, and the Party leaders had already decided that all of the candidates would be elected to office. The people were required to vote so that it would appear that they, the people, had a voice in government. Everyone was aware of this, and most of them did not even read the names on the election ballot as they completed it. A voter was permitted to cross out a candidate's name, but no one did that. What good would it have done? All the candidates were to be instated anyway.

The voting office would remain open until midnight, and at that time the election ballots were taken out of the ballot box and the votes were counted by the members of the commission. On the following day the election results in the village as well as the ballots were delivered to Kizil. The election results were also made known to the village people, but no one was interested. Everyone was sure that each candidate had received at least 99 per cent of all of the people's votes. They also knew that the newly elected officials would never oppose the Party leadership and so there would be no forthcoming political change. It is why I believe the people in the village rarely discussed politics. They felt powerless politically knowing that their votes would not change the system that controlled their lives.

In 1964 I was elected by the people to be a deputy on the Village Council. I was one of thirty deputies and in time I was chosen to serve on the Executive Committee of the Village Council. The Executive Committee was made up of five deputies. The entire Village Council would meet at least once in three months, but the Executive Committee would meet almost every week.

There were many problems to solve and many decisions to make. When the planting season approached, the Executive Committee would meet to plan the plowing and sowing campaigns. Decisions had to be made about the farm's livestock. The Village Council was responsible for the village school and hospital and the Executive Committee made sure that these two important institutions were run correctly. Being a member of the Executive Committee involved a lot of work, and I tried to be conscientious. I was proud to be a deputy and would remain a deputy until 1986.

One of my duties as a member of the Executive Committee was to conduct the wedding ceremonies in the village. I did this for more than twenty years. In preparation for a wedding the Village Club, which was where the wedding ceremonies took place, had to be decorated. That was my responsibility. I had to get musicians to play music, and I had to prepare a complimentary speech for the bride and groom. After giving my speech, I would ask the couple if they truly wanted to be married. If they said yes then I would announce to the audience the creation of a new family. I then told the couple to exchange wedding rings, an ancient Russian custom, and thereafter to kiss each other. After that I handed the couple a wedding certificate and gave them my best wishes.

When a couple had a child they would register their child with the Village Council. After several babies were registered, the Village Council would arrange a grand ceremony of registration which was to be held in the Village

Club on a future holiday. The ceremony was usually attended by the friends and relatives of the parents. It would begin with a speech of congratulations to the parents. As a member of the Village Council I was usually given that assignment. I would tell the new parents that their babies were fortunate to be born in a Communist country and that they would grow up and work in a happy and just society. Following the speech, the parents would be asked to walk to the front and onto the stage to receive their children's birth certificates. Each couple was also given a gift to remind them of this happy day. The registration ceremony was a wonderful tradition. It reflected a giving attitude that existed among the village people.

During my years as Village Council deputy, women would often ask me to help them with a variety of problems. One woman came to see me about her husband. She claimed that he was abusing her and asked me to go home with her and speak to him about this matter. She believed that I could persuade him to stop abusing her. On another occasion a woman told me that her husband was whipping her. I felt sorry for the woman and approached her husband about this matter. He admitted to whipping his wife but said he was doing it because he suspected her of being unfaithful to him.

When the State began cultivating the virgin lands of Kazakhstan and Siberia our village became involved. Unfortunately, the cultivation of the virgin lands ruined much of the steppes. The virgin land was plowed too deep, and this caused soil erosion. Why did they plow so deep? I suppose that this was a directive that came from the Central Committee of the Communist Party in Moscow or it might have come from the District Committee of the Communist Party in Kizil. I know that the District Committee would often decide when Izmaelovka should begin its sowing campaign and what seeds were to be planted. The men in the District Committee had no special knowledge in agriculture, yet they would tell the director of our farm, who was a professional agronomist, how to plant the seeds. The director of the farm would often ignore their orders, and he was reprimanded for doing so.

In 1964 I married my husband Victor Serafimovich. Victor was a tractor driver. He had been working on the farm since he was a little boy. His first job was as a herdsman, and then he cared for the village horses. After that he worked as a tractor driver, working from sunrise to sunset every day. Then he became a truck driver, and finally he worked as a truck crane operator. As a husband, Victor treated me well. He always supported my work as a librarian and as a deputy of the Village Council.

Our main source of livelihood was our kitchen garden and cow. The garden provided us with produce, and the cow gave us milk and a calf every year. We kept each calf for a year and then sold it for 300 rubles. We placed that money in the bank and added to those savings part of our monthly incomes.

Victor earned 75 rubles a month as a tractor driver, and as a librarian my monthly wage was 48 rubles. It was not much of an income, but we were frugal. The money we did spend was used to purchase sugar and candies at the village store. To tell you the truth, in the mid 1960s there was little else to buy in the store. In time, Victor and I had saved up enough money to purchase a motorcycle, and then after that we purchased an automobile. These purchases would not have been possible without our kitchen garden and our cow.

Our son Andrei was born in 1964. Two months after his birth, I was back at my job in the library. Since there was no nursery school on the farm, my mother agreed to take care of Andrei. She would come to our house in the morning, and then during my dinner break I would walk home to feed Andrei. I want to emphasize that it was mother who raised Andrei, and she would also raise my daughter Olga who was born in 1968. With my busy schedule as the village librarian and as a member of the Executive Committee of the Village Council, I was unable to spend much time with my children.

My workday began early in the morning. At 8:00 A.M. I would bring Andrei and Olga to school. Then I returned home to prepare breakfast for my husband. After that I would do some chores around the house. I was required to be in the library by 11:00 A.M., and shortly after I arrived I would write my report about the previous day. I recorded the number of people who visited the library, the types of books that had been checked out and the titles of the magazines and newspapers that the library had received. After that I put the books that had been returned to the library on the shelves. Then, if I had time, I would search for information in books or magazine about topics students or others had requested. By 4:00 P.M. I had returned to the village school to get my children and bring them to the library. Andrei and Olga liked to play in the library, and they would do that until it was time to go home. The library closed at 8:00 P.M.

Andrei finished his schooling the year that our country went to war in Afghanistan. The State tried to keep the war a secret. It was not reported to the village people on the radio or in the newspapers. We learned about the State's great secret from the parents whose sons were returned to their homes in coffins. I learned about the war from my sister, Nataly. She told me that a friend who had studied with her had been killed in Afghanistan. My sister did not learn about his death or that he had been sent to Afghanistan until after his body was returned home in a coffin. It was so typical of the State. The State would draft the young men and never tell their parents where they were sending their sons. Even the letters the parents received from their sons did not indicate their locations. A soldier's letter only revealed his unit number. No mother knew where her son was stationed, and then suddenly she would receive a "vikluchka."

Victor and I made sure that Andrei would not be called into the military. We were afraid that he would be sent to Afghanistan if he were drafted. I told Victor that if this should happen "I would never forgive myself." We knew that the State did not draft university students, but getting Andrei enrolled in a university would take time. We had to come up with an excuse to postpone his draft notice. The excuse we decided upon was an old head injury that Andrei had suffered while playing ice hockey. We then went to one of Victor's friends who worked at the recruiting office in Kizil, and he helped us delay Andrei's draft notice. Of course, Andrei did not know about our efforts, and if he had discovered what we were doing there would have been "a great war within our family." Andrei was not drafted, and eventually he entered the university and graduated in 1988 with a degree in engineering.

A person who did not want to attend a university could earn a degree by taking correspondence courses. The first step toward doing that was getting the village leaders to write a letter of recommendation to the university administrators. Then the person had to take and pass an entrance examination given by the university. After that the student was given reading and writing assignments for each of several courses. The assignments, when completed, were sent to the university. If they had been done satisfactorily, the student received an invitation to take an examination on each course in which the assignments had been completed. It required that the student travel to the university. The expense of the trip was paid by the Village Council. If the student passed the examinations, the process would be repeated with another block of courses. When all the required courses were completed, the student was awarded a diploma.

In the 1980s the people lost respect for the government of our country. The people became better informed about their leaders, and it was obvious to them that the leaders within the Communist Party enjoyed a higher standard of living than most of the citizens within the Soviet Union. The Communist leadership owned cars, they had their own hospitals, they did their shopping in special stores and they were able to purchase goods that were unavailable to the general populace. Even the regional Party leader behaved like a Russian tsar. He made himself inaccessible and unapproachable. His behavior was reflective of the way our government viewed the people. They treated us as peasants, feeding us with their stupid slogans believing that we would naively accept them and work hard so that they could live in luxury.

When Mikhail Gorbachev became the leader of our country, we prayed that God would give him good health and the strength to carry out the kind of reforms that would improve life for all the people. Initially, Gorbachev did not disappoint us. We admired his report devoted to the fortieth anniversary of our country's victory over fascist Germany. We were thankful that he ended Soviet Russia's participation in the war in Afghanistan. We were happy that he improved relations with the United States. Sometimes Victor and I would stay up until three in the morning to listen to a speech Gorbachev had made the previous day. We had never experienced such a clever leader as Gorbachev. All of our past leaders had been too old and inept. Breznev, for example, would mumble when he made a speech on television (see Glossary— Brezhnev, Leonid). We could not understand what he said. Then there was Andropov who was always sick and let us not forget Chernenko who was barely alive. With Gorbachev, we finally had a genuine leader and one who told the people the truth, so we thought.

The disappointment came later after Gorbachev started "perestroika." Suddenly the consumer goods disappeared from the stores. The shelves in the store in Izmaelovka and in the stores of Magnitogorsk became empty. It became difficult to find a staple product such as cereal. I remember that on one occasion as I entered the village store the shop girl told me secretly that they had just received a new supply of rice. She agreed to sell me several kilograms. I was so happy. After I brought the rice home, I hid it in the cellar. During my next visit to the store I bought some millet and hid that as well. When the store received an order of soaps and washing powders I, along with many others, stood in line listening to the people discuss the economic situation of our country. No one blamed Gorbachev for our difficulties. They believed that Gorbachev did not know about our economic hardships. They all liked Gorbachev. The year was 1988, and I bought so much soap during that year that I am still using the soap.

"Glasnost" was another policy started by Gorbachev. Under this policy the people were theoretically given the right to talk more openly in public. In reality, we were permitted to voice only what the authorities wanted to hear. Even now we can speak openly, but we must be careful not to anger the leaders.

In 1992 our paper money lost almost all of its value. Who could have predicted that the price of products would rise so high? We believed that it was possible for prices to increase by ten times, but we never expected them to rise by ten thousand times. It happened to the price of bread, and it took place in one year. The salaries were increased as well, once every three months, but they could not keep up with the rising rate of inflation. Because of this, our savings were wiped out.

We were accustomed to great difficulties in Izmaelovka, but we had never suffered from the terrible effects of an unstable economy. Many of us agreed that living under the old economic system had been better. Under the new system we felt lost. The shock was so severe that it affected our health. The changes were particularly hard on the men in the village. The changes drove them to drinking. I think they turned to vodka because they lost hope for gaining a better life. There were people who looked at this development and concluded that the village is dying. I believe that their assessment is correct.

Conclusion

What has happened to Izmaelovka? What has become of the people who labored in its fields and buildings back when it was a collective farm? Valentina Nenasheva believes that the village is dying. The tannery in Izmaelovka where the hides of the village cows were once prepared is no longer in operation. The warm high fitting boots and beautiful coats made of the wool sheared from the village sheep and sold in cities such as Magnitogorsk are no longer being produced. The small factory in which state farm wheat was made into macaroni and sold in the village store and outside of the village has been closed. Subbotniks that were designed to beautify the village are no longer being conducted. Socialist competitions are only a memory, and the village main street is no longer the Avenue of Honor graced on one side with large photographs of the most productive workers within Izmaelovka. The steel rectangular frames that held the photographs stand empty, and some have become damaged. The large statue of Vladimir Lenin made of cement and standing directly in front of the Village Club is beginning to crack and deteriorate. The busts of Vladimir Lenin, Karl Marx and Friedrich Engels that once had prominent places within the main room of the village administrative building have been removed and are kept in a small storage room in the rear of the building. Many of the residents hope that the village will one day again have a beautiful Russian Orthodox Church, but there is no money for its construction. The people earn barely enough income to pay for their expenses. They are experiencing hard times and Izmaelovka's economic setback has resulted in a number of people leaving the village out of necessity. Valentina and the other six women who are the subjects of this book still reside in Izmaelovka. They are frugal and have secured for themselves lifestyles with which they are satisfied.

Glossary of Names, Titles, Terms, Abbreviations and Events

Brezhnev, Leonid. In mid-October 1964 the people of the Soviet Union learned that Nikita Khrushchev had been removed from power and succeeded by two members of the Presidium. Leonid Brezhnev replaced him as First Secretary of the Communist Party and A.N. Kosygin became Premier (chairman of the Council of Ministers). Both were Khrushchev men. It was, however, Brezhnev who would dominate the Soviet Union for almost two decades.

brigade. A work brigade was made up of men and women and was directed by a brigade leader. On a collective farm each brigade was assigned a work detail such as plowing an agricultural field or harvesting a wheat field with tractors and combines.

Chelyabinsk. Chelyabinsk dates back to the eighteenth century when it was established as a military settlement and a place to which political exiles were sent. It would remain a place of detainment in the early nineteen hundreds, and well known Bolsheviks such as Joseph Stalin were sent to Chelyabinsk prison. After the Trans-Siberian Railroad was completed a town would grow around the Chelyabinsk train station, but it was during the First Five-Year Plan that Chelyabinsk would grow into a large industrial center. An electrolyte-zinc plant and a machine-tools manufacturing plant were built. The city would eventually boast the world's largest tractor factory producing most of the tractors that were used on the collective farms and state farms in Siberia.

Cossacks. During the sixteenth and seventeenth centuries Russians moved east beyond the Ural Mountains to the Pacific Ocean. The frontiersmen known as Cossacks led the way. The term Cossack was derived from a Tartar word "Kazakh" meaning free man, but in time it came to mean anyone who lived on the steppe fringe of southern Russia.

druzka. A groom will have a male friend check the bed sheets for bloodstains after he has spent the first night with his wife. The male friend is the druzka.

Gagarin, Yuri. On April 12, 1961, the Soviet scientists astounded the world by sending the first human being into orbit around the earth. His name was Yuri Gagarin.

Great Patriotic War. Soviet Union citizens called World War Two, the Great Patriotic War.

Great Purge. Joseph Stalin's campaign of mass arrests and executions in the late 1930s is called the Great Purge and was triggered on December 1, 1933, the day that Sergei Kirov, the Communist Party chief of Leningrad, was assassinated in Leningrad. The assassin, Leonid Nikolaev, a disgruntled former Party member, was arrested and shot. The story that Stalin himself had plotted the assassination has not been confirmed, but he did use the incident to launch a reign of terror. He responded to the incident by issuing new laws against terrorists. Henceforth, they were neither allowed the services of a defense lawyer nor permitted appeals. Those who were sentenced to death were to be executed immediately. Within the next several months, thousands of people were arrested. The relatives of Nikolaev were among those who were arrested, and they too were executed. Arresting and executing family members of those found guilty of committing crimes against the Soviet Union became a policy enforced by the State during the Great Purge.

In 1936 the Great Purge began. The official story was that Trotskyite agitation abroad was linked with the murder of Kirov and with alleged plans for the murder of Stalin. A series of public political trials took place. In the first (1936), sixteen prominent Bolsheviks were found guilty of being involved in the Kirov assassination and were executed. In the second (1937), seventeen other leading Bolsheviks confessed that they had knowledge of a conspiracy between Leon Trotsky and the German and Japanese intelligence services by which Russian territory was to be transferred to Germany and Japan. Thirteen of the accused were shot, and the other four were given sentences and died several years later. Stalin also turned on the leadership of the Red Army. It too was accused of being in league with the Soviet Union's enemies, Germany and Japan. The military commanders refused to confess, but Stalin had them shot in June and July 1937. Their executions were made public after the event.

The last of the public trials were conducted in March 1938. The accused involved a wide range of victims that included two old Bolsheviks. They were charged with several crimes which included conspiring with Trotsky, Germany, Japan, Great Britain and Poland to dismember the Soviet Union. Most of the victims were found guilty and executed.

The Great Purge involved much more than the public trials of prominent Bolsheviks and the trials of Soviet military commanders. Two vice-commissars of foreign affairs and most of the ambassadors of the diplomatic corps, fifty of the seventy-one members of the Central Committee of the Communist Party, almost all the military judges who sat in judgment of and condemned the military commanders, two successive heads of the secret police and the prime ministers and chief officials of all the non-Russian Soviet Republics were killed or vanished. Thousands of engineers, scientists, industrial managers, scholars, artists and common citizens disappeared. The local units of Stalin's secret police were even ordered to arrest a certain percentage of the people in their districts. Anyone might be awakened in the middle of the night by the knock on the door of a NKVD officer and be charged with committing "crimes against the people." The arrests of the victims left their survivors with the reminder that they must submit to the will of the Communist Party and its leader or suffer the consequences. In 1939 as many as ten million Soviet citizens were being held in corrective labor camps, and by this time some three million had already died as a result of the purges.

Hero of Socialist Labor. It was a title that was given to a Soviet worker who through her or his work made an exceptional contribution to the construction of Communism in the Soviet Union.

icon. An icon in the Russian Orthodox Church is generally an image of Jesus the son of God or the Virgin Mary or some other saint that has been painted on a small or large smoothed wooden panel. The Church teaches that a saint in heaven will hear the requests that are expressed in prayers by a worshiper, and the requests are then brought by the saint to Jesus or God. An icon bearing the image of a saint is designed to assist the worshiper by helping her or him visualize the saint.

KGB. Komit Gosudarstvennoy Bezopasnosti (Committee for State Security) The security police force from 1954 to 1991 was commonly called the KGB.

Khrushchev, Nikita. Following Stalin's death the Soviet Union was guided initially by a collective leadership of top Communists. Georgi Malenkov who had been close to Stalin succeeded him as Premier and Nikita Khrushchev became the First Secretary (a position that Stalin had called General Secretary) of the Communist Party. As the principle leader, Malenkov emphasized the production of consumer goods and pledged to raise markedly the people's living standards. Malenkov would soon be challenged by Khrushchev and in early 1955 Malenkov was forced to resign as Premier and Nikolai Bulganin became the new Premier. In March Khrushchev succeeded Bulganin as Premier and in September Khrushchev was the undisputed leader within the Communist Party.

Khrushchev's virgin lands program. Nikita Khrushchev embarked on an extensive virgin lands program to increase wheat production. More than 40,500 hectares (100,000 acres) of prairie lands in the Ural region, Kazakhstan and Siberia were cultivated. The program initially increased grain production to a new record high, but the applied farming techniques proved inappropriate for the soil and the new agricultural lands soon underwent severe erosion.

Khrushchev's speech to the Twentieth Century Congress. At the Twentieth Century Congress of the Communist Party held in February 1956, Nikita Khrushchev gave a long speech in which he denounced Joseph Stalin. He described in detail to startled Communist delegates the horrible acts of cruelty that were committed at the orders of Stalin during the purges of the 1930s. Thousands of devoted Communists had been liquidated and many top military leaders had been executed, which weakened gravely the Red Army. He accused Stalin of trusting Hitler and jeopardizing the country's defense. He claimed that Stalin's wartime failings caused the deaths of countless Soviet troops. Further, Khrushchev explained how Stalin had "supported the glorification of his own person with all conceivable methods." The speech left many delegates in a state of shock and as details of the speech became known to the Soviet public, there were other responses. Many people were distressed at the attack on the man they had worshipped so long. There were also many who were not surprised; they had suspected that Stalin was something less than godlike.

Komsomol. Membership in the Komsomol (The Young Communist League) was less extensive than in the Young Pioneers. Only about one-third of the young people between the ages of fifteen and twenty-eight became members. However, Komsomol membership among students in institutions of higher learning was usually high because membership would help a person gain admission into these institutions. Although the age limit for membership was twenty-eight, provision was made in the Komsomol statutes for officers to remain in the organization beyond that age.

Komsomol members were exposed to intense ideological indoctrination and were expected to participate in all aspects of Soviet society. Members would offer their services to the armed forces if the State called for recruits in an emergency situation. They were also expected to work in a factory or on a collective farm whenever there was a shortage of labor. Members who entered the military or who joined an industrial or agricultural force were responsible for the political education of their co-workers who were of the same age group. Members had been trained for this responsibility during Komsomol meetings, which were mainly discussions and lectures on Marxist-Leninist ideology.

Komsomol members performed an important surveillance function in society. They frequently inspected enterprises and did this usually without prior warning. They sought to expose corruption, waste and inefficiency in management and laziness and tardiness among workers. The surveillance function of the Komsomol was even more extensive in institutions of higher learning. The activities of students who were members were carefully observed. Failure to conform to Komsomol standards of behavior could result in expulsion from the organization. Komsomol members with a university education were an important source for recruitment for the Communist Party. Membership in the Komsomol did not, however, ensure that a person would be admitted to the Party.

kopek. It is a monetary unit. One hundred kopeks are equal in value to one ruble.

Luxemburg, Rosa. Born in Russian Poland in 1871, Rosa Luxemburg became a Marxist political theorist, socialist, philosopher and revolutionary. In 1916 she co-founded the Spartacus League which two years later became the German Communist Party.

Magnitogorsk. Magnitogorsk came into existence after Stalin commissioned that the world's largest and most advanced steel mill be built east of the Ural Mountains. Between the founding of the city in 1929 and the year1932 the site grew from a few hundred to 250,000 people. Many of its early residents were Kulaks who were brought here after their farms were expropriated during collectivization. A large number of residents were criminals. There were also idealists who had come voluntarily believing that their efforts would help build a Marxist socialist state. Together these people labored under extremely adverse working conditions for low wages. They lived in inadequate housing without running water or a sewerage system and were provided few medical facilities. The Magnitogorsk Steel Works was completed in less than ten years, and it became the largest producer of steel in the Soviet Union.

NKVD. Narodnyy Konissariat Vnutrennikh Del (People's Commissariat of Internal Affairs) The People's Commissariat for Internal Affairs was the organization that Stalin placed in charge to carry out the Great Purge of the 1930s, but it was better known as NKVD. Its origin was in CHEKA which was disbanded once the Civil War (1918–21) ended and the threat of domestic and foreign opposition to Lenin and his Communists had receded. The functions of CHEKA were transferred in 1922 to the State Political Administration, or GPU, which was less powerful than its predecessor. In 1923 the Unified State Political Administration, or OGPU, was created and during its tenure, which ended in 1934, repression against the people lessened. The secret police again acquired vast punitive powers when it became, in

1934, the People's Commissariat for Internal Affairs, or NKVD. It was not subject to Party control or restricted by law. The NKVD was the direct instrument of Stalin for use against people in the Party and country that he wanted purged. In the end the people who did the purging were also purged. They were used as scapegoats by Stalin for the horrendous acts that they had committed at his commands.

October Revolution. Vladimir Lenin and his Bolsheviks removed from power the Provisional Government on November 7, 1917, according to the Gregorian calendar. The removal was called the October Revolution. In Russia the Gregorian calendar was accepted after the October Revolution (so named because it took place in October 1917 in the Julian calendar). On January 24, 1918, the Council of People's Commissars decreed that January 31, 1918, was to be followed by February 14, 1918.

Pugachev, Emelyan. Emelyan Pugachev's revolt took place during the reign of Catherine II also known as "the Great." Pugachev (1726–75) was a Cossack who in his youth had been a military adventurer. Disappointed in his career, he made his way to the Ural Mountains where he recruited tribesmen and laborers who were being forced to work in the mines. In 1773, Pugachev proclaimed that he was Tsar Peter III, the murdered husband of Catherine II. Pugachev claimed that he had escaped the clutches of Catherine and was resolved to give the peasants liberty from serfdom and ownership of land. He began his uprising with small raiding parties against local landlords and military outposts and soon gained the allegiance of thousands of peasants. In 1774, with an army of nearly twenty thousand people, Pugachev captured the city of Kazan and threatened to advance on Moscow. It was another year before Catherine the Great's forces crushed the rebellion. Pugachev was captured, was brought to Moscow and was executed.

ruble. The ruble is a monetary unit, divided into 100 kopeks.

svakha. She, representing a young man, will announce to a young woman the young man's desire to marry her.

svashka. A bride will have a female friend check the bed sheets for bloodstains after she has spent the first night with her husband. The female friend is the svashka.

svat. He, representing another young man, will announce to a young woman the young man's desire to marry her.

Victory Day. May 9 is Victory Day, and the Soviet citizens celebrated the end of the Great Patriotic War on this day.

vikluchka. It was an official notification sent to the family of a soldier who had died.

Young Pioneers. Within the framework of the educational system students in the Soviet Union joined youth organizations that were sanctioned by the Communist Party. These organizations included the Young Octoberists for children between the ages of six and nine and the Young Pioneers for children between the ages of nine and fifteen. Each school had a staff member who was to administer the activities of the Young Pioneers. Each class was a detachment of Young Pioneers that was comprised of three to five units, and the detachment was led by a Komsomol member. The leaders of the Young Pioneers worked closely with the classroom teachers to teach the children to be conscientious students and good citizens. Nearly all recreational activities for the Young Pioneers took place under the auspices of the organization. The programs that the organization sponsored ranged from sports to scouting activities to folk dancing and ballet lessons. Most communities had facilities for these activities and there were Young Pioneer camps throughout the country. Young Pioneers were exposed to ideological indoctrination, but it was usually limited to instilling patriotism and Soviet values. Intensive ideological indoctrination was reserved for the members of the Komsomol.

zatiruka. It is a soup made with wheat flour and potatoes. Some leek and other green leaf vegetables may be added to the soup.

Bibliography

Clarkson, Jesse D. A History of Russia. New York: Random House, Inc., 1961.

Moss, Walter G. A History of Russia. New York: The McGraw-Hill Companies, Inc., 1997.

Payne, Robert. The Life and Death of Lenin. New York: Simon and Schuster, Inc., 1964.

Werth, Alexander. Russia at War 1941-1945. New York: E.P. Dutton and Co., Inc., 1964.

About the Authors

Alexey Vinogradov was born in Leningrad, USSR. He earned his Ph.D. in Archaeology from Leningrad State University. He is the coauthor of The Battle for Leningrad published in 2005 by St. Petersburg State University Press. Alexey is Dean of the Research Center for Archaeology, Historical Sociology and Cultural Heritage at St. Petersburg State University, St. Petersburg, Russia.

Albert Pleysier was born in Utrecht, the Netherlands and immigrated to the United States. He earned his Ph.D. in History from West Virginia University. Albert is the coauthor of two books: The Battle for Leningrad published in Russian by St. Petersburg State University Press and Surviving the Blockade of Leningrad published by University Press of America. He is a professor of History at Piedmont College in Demorest, Georgia.